Lesley Black could hardly claim that sea-faring is in her blood, having been born and raised in Welwyn Garden City — a town more famed as the home of Shredded Wheat than as a yachtsman's Mecca. Nevertheless, after an uncertain start, she now admits to an addiction to the sport and adds that, just as people grow to be like their pets, over the years she has grown to be more and more like her boat — sturdy, well built, if slightly worn around the edges, temperamental at times but capable of impressive performance if handled with due respect. And also like the boat, her skipper insists with feeling, she demands a lot of attention and is expensive to maintain.

She, the skipper, and their two junior hands live in Northern Ireland from whence they cruise regularly in their 35-foot yawl 'Mary Lunn', as members of Quoile Yacht Club of Strangford Lough, and of the Irish Cruising Club.

Must I go down to the sea again?

Lesley Black
illustrated by Mike Peyton

ADLARD COLES LIMITED
8 Grafton Street, London W1

Fernhurst Books

Adlard Coles Ltd
William Collins Sons & Co. Ltd
8 Grafton Street, London W1X 3LA

First published in Great Britain by
Fernhurst Books 1983
Paperback edition published by Adlard Coles Ltd/
Fernhurst Books 1985

Copyright © Fernhurst Books 1983

British Library Cataloguing in Publication Data
Black, Lesley
Must I go down to the sea again?
1. Sailing—Anecdotes, facetiae, satire, etc.
I. Title
797.1'24'0207   GV811

ISBN 0-229-11767-8

Printed and bound in Great Britain by
Billing & Sons Limited, Worcester

Contents

1

A toe in the water

I don't suffer from coy reticence when it comes to recounting my early sailing experiences. For one thing, what was horrific at the time can seem pretty hilarious when viewed from a comfortable distance. Secondly, confession of one's own ineptitude encourages others to dredge up memories that they have kept firmly under psychological wraps, with some rather revealing results.

Why is it, I wonder, that so many skippers when attempting to induct a newcomer into the sport — especially if the newcomer is female — insist on employing the 'throw 'em in at the deep end' technique? The husband of a friend of mine, who'd got his own sailing colours by a gentle progression from the dinghy fleet, eventually invested the family savings in a fast, sleek racing machine for which, of course, he required extra crew in the shape of his wife. In his eyes, the ideal day for her first outing was a grey, squally one, with rain and mist thrown in for good measure.

"Give you a great chance to see how the boat performs," he eagerly assured her.

As soon as they were out of the sheltering headlands of the anchorage, the wind laid the yacht flat on her ear and my pal, with an agility that gave her skipper a great chance to see how *she* could perform, scrambled onto the weather deck, lodged herself firmly between the shrouds and stayed there for the

duration, with only the odd whimper escaping from her clenched lips to betray her inner turmoil.

A doctor I know tells me that he's never yet met a woman who could take with equanimity to a boat heeling — according to him we can't accept these sudden stomach-heaving lurches from the vertical in the same way men do. It's something to do with a woman's psychological make-up, he says; I reckon he's got a point, we've always been more level-headed than men. Obviously he had this in mind when he decided to buy a catamaran to give his wife her first taste of the sea. He was quick to point out that catamarans didn't heel, which boosted her confidence no end, but neglected to add that when making to windward, they slam up and down with a motion that emulsifies the brain and shakes your gold fillings loose. She found that out for herself, and she didn't like it.

The motorboat enthusiasts aren't immune to problems of this type either. I once saw a couple bringing a small cruiser, unused and gleaming, down the slipway. He, struggling under the weight, was immaculate in pale blue with peaked cap and pipe like a model from a tobacco advert, while she was all box pleats, silk scarf and sunspecs — a sort of nautical Jackie Onassis.

"I'm getting on board," she trilled. "I must be on board for the launching!"

"On you go then, my love," he cried, as heartily as the pipe would allow.

But barely had her strap-sandalled foot touched the cockpit sole when he stepped on a particularly large and juicy chunk of seaweed, a denim-clad bottom slapped painfully onto the concrete and he lost control of the trolley. Boat and lady careered on into the waves while ear-shattering screams rent the morning stillness.

"A rope! Throw me a rope!" he bawled. She grabbed one, neatly hanked, and hurled it at him with both surprising strength and stunning accuracy as it caught him on the side of the head and laid him flat again.

"You bloody fool, not *both* ends," he wailed. When last seen she was making good time, stern first and sobbing hysterically, for the sandbank (dries 3 ft) in the middle of the bay.

Not that we were really in any position to laugh. When we launched our very first sailing vessel — a Scorpion dinghy by breed — we'd been told all about rigging her ashore and getting the sails ready for action, but nobody had mentioned how sheets get themselves jammed and twisted in knots during this process. We got her off the trolley easily enough — in fact one of the wheels sneakily nosed its way over the side of the slipway

Lodged herself firmly between the shrouds . . .

and she fell off — but then a playful gust filled the mainsail and if the skipper hadn't put in a swift racing crawl demonstration, fully clothed, we'd have had a Marie Celeste situation on our hands.

But the biggest snag with this new venture was that, once launched, neither of us had the least idea of how to sail — a fact which the skipper would rather have died (possibly by drowning) than admit.

Men in general nurse a conviction that they have an innate understanding of all things nautical which, however deeply hidden, will somehow surface whenever needed. Certainly they seem to pick up the jargon with amazing ease. Within hours my skipper was able to bark out orders which sounded completely authentic but were totally incomprehensible to me — and, I strongly suspect, to him. "You hank on the genoa while I reeve this halyard" may make sense to a well versed OSTAR man but provokes only a blank stare from a crewperson who doesn't know a snap-shackle from a Turk's head.

So although he could vastly impress the throng of weekend sightseers with his yelled commands, if the skipper actually wanted a job done he had to revert to more normal parlance. But since "clip these metal thingammies over the wire at the front end" doesn't quite have that deep-sea ring about it, he'd deliver such utterances in a sly mutter out of the corner of his mouth, which did little to improve the lines of communication. We'd depart the quayside in an atmosphere of confusion and mutual hostility — hardly an encouraging start in a sport that was supposed to bring us into close, working harmony.

Somehow, for reasons which defy analysis, we did eventually get our act into gear and then, of course, we became overconfident and — worse still — scathing in our attitudes towards others. With newfound bravado, we abandoned our well rehearsed technique of dropping all sail about a mile out and paddling, Sanders-of-the-River style, for the slipway when our time was up, and instead went for the more spectacular approach under sail. Until, that is, the day we did our run in at a speed we hadn't quite anticipated — the gentle breeze having turned into a hearty blow while we were out discussing alimony and the custody of the children at the third racing buoy. It was a stroke of cruel fate that a blue-jeaned powerboat enthusiast, the lowest of the low in our élitist estimation, had

10

chosen that moment to undertake his launch. We came hurtling in just as his 'reckless burner-up of precious fossil fuels' reached the end of the slip.

"Let fly everything!" bawled my frenzied hero, and I, faithful to the end, freed off both sheets and halyards with lightning speed. Totally enshrouded in yards of flapping terylene, looking and sounding like a pair of avenging visitations from the spirit world, we charged blindly on. It was truly astounding to see how large, and expensive, a hole our stem-head made in his polished topsides.

Despite our inauspicious start, we were quick to progress up the yachting ladder and join the ranks of keelboat owners, and soon 'Flora', a twenty-three foot one-offer of uncertain pedigree, entered our lives. For us, she was not a happy ship. My first and last outing in her ended abruptly when her main gooseneck jammed at precisely the same second that her outboard engine elected to leap into the water, and all while we were trying to weave a discreet path through the massed start of the local 505 championships. We had to go off on holiday while the resultant flak died down, and weren't all that surprised on our return to find that 'Flora' must also have felt some embarrassment, as only the tip of her mast, with token seagull attached, was visible at our mooring. It was not, as we at first suspected, sabotage by enraged dinghy racers that caused the sinking, but a brisk southwesterly and an insecure porthole.

The lull that ensued, through financial necessity, was restful but brief. In vain I tried to interest the skipper in golf, indoor bowling, snooker and petit-point embroidery; but in truth my heart wasn't in it. I'd already joined in, I'd actually enjoyed the odd five minutes here and there; I was, to all intents, hooked and landed.

My newfound commitment did not, alas, mean that all was harmony on board. I had thought that on our boat we were pretty good at talking things through and making joint decisions based on sensible compromise, until the day I heard

11

my skipper being asked if he would mind sailing on the Committee Boat for some Club outing or other.

"Why should I mind? I always sail on a bloody committee boat," he growled, with some feeling.

When we began cruising with some degree of earnestness, we were aware there might be tensions so we decided to let them work themselves out in sheltered waters before attempting anything too ambitious. It all went very smoothly too, as well it should, for our home ground — Strangford Lough in beautiful County Down — is well protected from the worst of the weather. And while there's plenty of space and just enough rocks and islets to make life interesting, it's also small enough for the nervous sailor to know that yacht club, well-stocked bar, and the safety of one's own mooring chain are rarely more than an hour's sailing (or for the non-purist, half an hour's motoring) away.

My first inkling that cruising wasn't always like that came when, on the promise of a night's indulgences at the Isle of Man hot-spots, I was lured out through the tide-swept narrows to cross the Irish Sea. A slight misreading of the tide tables, plus a fresh onshore wind, led to my high spirits being rapidly dispelled as we arrived at the bar (nautical variety with attendant overfalls) at what was decidedly the wrong moment. Our sturdy 27-footer, till now of staid and biddable temperament, showed new character as she rose, flopped down and wallowed viciously in steep waves. The baby, who had been snoring happily in her carrycot on the saloon floor, began to raise startled eyes above the rim as she was lifted bodily from the mattress and plonked down again with sharp expulsions of breath. The senior child, then about six, attempted for ostrich-like reasons of his own to climb headfirst into one of the cockpit lockers, emitting strident cries of "don't like it, don't like it!"

Vaguely aware that a stirring song was supposed to help in times of stress I cast around for a suitable ditty but the only one that sprang to mind was 'Old Father Thames'. The crew of the fancy gin palace that creamed past at full throttle, helping us

12

. . . only the tip of her mast, with token seagull attached, was visible.

not one bit with her towering wake, must have been somewhat puzzled to see the green-faced figure at our stern bawling lustily that she was "High in the hills, Low in the vales, Careless and fancy free" while clasping a small child in a half-nelson and beating time with a pink plastic rattle.

I do feel that men could show their crews more consideration than they do. Terrified by Women's Libbers into nightmares of emasculation and determined to retain their macho image at all costs, they flatly refuse to acknowledge any lapses of confidence and retreat behind a smokescreen of bluff heartiness and manly strength.

Let a few similar types get together and the problem is magnified a hundred times. There have been many occasions when we, in company with other hapless mariners, have

13

thrashed our way through head winds, rain, hail and violent seas and into the blessed calm of a sheltered harbour. Limp, shaking and whey-faced, we have scarcely tied up at the quayside before the skippers are all up on deck indulging in riotous laughter and exchanging dismissive cracks about "a fine sailing breeze" and "a little bit of a chop out there". The women, meanwhile, tightlipped and grim, are down below retrieving scattered belongings, pacifying crazed children, hunting out the brandy bottle, or consulting the pilot book for the nearest rail-link to home and sanity.

A pal of mine once had a long, hard sail from Wales to the Irish haven of Kinsale. It had been cold, wet and wearying, and it was well into the small hours when they tied up thankfully at the almost deserted marina and turned in for a well earned kip. So she was not a bit pleased to wake early next morning to the sound of raised voices, her own skipper's prominent amongst them, noisy revelry and the unmistakable popping of corks. In a blaze of fury she threw back the hatch cover and let them have it with both barrels.

"What the hell do you think you're doing holding a party at this time of day?" she screamed at the assembled company scattered about the several large craft that now surrounded hers. "Have you no consideration for people who actually do some *sailing*? Don't you realise that some of us have just been at sea for nearly *thirty hours*?"

And she slammed back the hatch and retired to her bunk, leaving behind a stunned silence. It was several hours before her husband dared venture below again, and even then he thought it prudent not to tell her that the gentlemen who had so thoughtlessly disturbed her slumbers were in fact the winning crews in a just-completed race — from Newport, Rhode Island, USA.

2

Dressed over-all

When my pal delivered her broadside to those transatlantic voyagers much of its impact was due to the fact that the portion of her anatomy she thrust through the forehatch was totally starkers, her sleeping bag not having risen from the bunk as rapidly as she did. Mercifully, such incidents are rare, but the choice of clothing for even the more normal sailing scene brings its own headaches.

When packing gear for a cruise it's a toss-up between listening to the voice of optimism, which says that a skimpy bikini or two and large bottle of tanning oil will fill the bill admirably, or heeding the warnings of bitter experience, which insist on a plentiful supply of thick sweaters, stout trousers and long johns. True pessimists would add a full set of that ravishingly attractive thermal underwear which extends from neck to ankle, gives you a body temperature only a degree below sauna-bath level, and produces itches in places a lady doesn't scratch. The only thing you can be sure of is that, whatever you bring, you won't have enough locker space for it.

Even for women who like nothing better than preening in front of fitting-room mirrors, shopping for such garments cannot be regarded as a pleasure. Few and far between are the chandlers who waste valuable shop space on pandering to the vanity of their customers. Proper display stands are rare, and if they do exist are often so overloaded with haphazardly arranged goods that any attempt to turn them round to find approximately the right size leads to an avalanche of wire coat hangers and navy blue wool.

Ask the whereabouts of the fitting room and you'll be treated to a raised eyebrow and a hollow laugh. If you're lucky you'll be shown into a converted broom cupboard, with brushes, buckets and teetering pile of cardboard boxes still in residence, or perhaps reluctantly offered the use of the manager's office, with no mirror, a desk piled high with bills, letters of complaint and dirty coffee cups, and a persistently ringing phone. At worst it'll be, "Here you are, love. Just nip behind the wellie-boot stand and I'll look the other way." You're condemned to an embarrassing session of heaving, sweating and glancing over your shoulder, hoping all the while that you put on the bra without the safety pins that morning.

If there *is* a mirror, it's always at the wrong end of the shop where the skippers are trying on their trendy headgear, deciding which cap gives them the greatest air of authority, or (if they're honest) makes them look least like a displaced zoo keeper. The reflecting surface will be at the wrong height, and almost obscured by stickers advertising engine oil, fishing rods or the date, venue and course to sail of last year's Soling Championships. The sailing woman is forced to trail the length of the building under the critical gaze of a gathering of would-be Chichesters and present herself to her skipper's scrutiny decked out in yards of ill-fitting, brilliant orange vinyl and a sou'wester several sizes too big.

"I always recommend going for a larger size in oilskins," purrs the wily salesman, knowing full well he hasn't got a 'Small' in the place. "Then you can wear a big, warm sweater underneath — and I just happen to have a nice line in pure wool, Breton stripe, if only I can find them . . ."

Faced with such an apparition the wise skipper will bite back the amusing comments that spring to his lips or else he'll be treated to a flurry of hastily ripped-off clothing, a brief and to-the-point dissertation on exactly what he can do with himself

16

and his boat, a lingering whiff of car exhaust fumes as she departs the scene and hefty bill for flowers and French perfume to restore the status quo. Plus, of course, the need to eat large helpings of humble pie or else seek out a crew of less sensitive nature.

Even so, I reckon it's still worth the effort to go out and do your own choosing. If not you may find that your skipper, mindful of the painful recriminations he'll have to bear when his lady has her favourite leisurewear ruined by salt water, diesel, and baked-bean juice, will do it for you. Some women consider this a smart idea, on the grounds that if he wants them to go sailing then he can jolly well foot the bill, but I would dispute that. It's such an unpleasant shock to find, on your birthday, that the gold bracelet and luxury cashmere jumper you've been hinting about for weeks have materialised as a pair of sweat-proof socks, business-like wellies and a safety harness. My smart alternative is to do my own shopping and put it all on his account. Just let him try to raise any objections, that's all.

Making your choice from the gear on offer can be very much a hit-and-miss affair. If you haven't sailed much, how are you to know whether waist-high or chest-high trousers are best for a lady, for example? My preference, for what it's worth, is chest-highs. The waist-highs, if they are to stay up during the action, must have a fairly constricting band around the middle — fine if you're one of the snake-hipped males the designers have in mind, but for a lady with fine, child-bearing hips they mean a lot of wriggling, panting and holding of breath. Chest-highs slide on and off with ease, vital for a lady wanting the loo in a hurry, and also give more protection, provided you don't mind an outline like Coco the Clown.

And what about the top half? Buy a zip-up jacket and you run the risk of water seeping in somewhere down the front — and it's amazing how many pints you can collect in your undies through just a tiny stitching hole. If you go instead for the over-the-head smock style you either have to carry a bag of hairdressing equipment with you on each trip ashore or walk around looking like the high priestess of punk.

Then there is the all-in-one design. These too are easy to get on and off (just as well, since a call of nature requires a total strip for ladies) but they are once again made with the lanky male in mind. On a woman, the excess material hangs in baggy bits that squeak when you walk and adds inches to those areas you'd like to play down. Stick a bobble hat on top and you have all the pulse-quickening sex appeal of Andy Pandy.

One aspect of this male-orientated design which benefits women is, oddly enough, the discreet little zip in the trouser front. It's useless as far as its intended purpose goes, of course, but it does come in very handy in allowing a modicum of extra

Reluctantly offered the use of the manager's office . . .

breathing space when the sailing menu has added unwanted poundage to the form divine. And it will, I promise you — even the most strong-willed find it hard to stay sylphlike on a continued diet of doorstep sandwiches, quick-cook pasta and mountains of instant spud.

For under-the-oilies clothing, the experts recommend several layers of lightweight garments rather than one all-enveloping jumper. This is sound thinking, until you come to do the ship's laundry. On our boat this has to be accomplished in a minute bucket, with the skipper breathing down my neck and complaining loudly about the amount of fresh water being 'wasted' on the idle luxury of clean clothes. I've found that to say, "I'm just giving this one jumper a quick sluice" raises far fewer hackles than, "I've done three shirts, four polo-necks and two vests and there's still your combinations and all the socks to go." Even if he relents, and maybe allows me an extra bucket of rinsing water, he's still less than tolerant about his sleek pride and joy being converted to a sea-going slum with dripping, greyish unmentionables festooned from every available stretch of rigging.

But like it or not, the washing must be done because on any prolonged cruise the pong factor cannot be ignored. This is the inevitable result of having active, over-clad and often tension-filled bodies trapped within waterproof coverings for any length of time. The aromas produced could only be considered acceptable, and even then with a certain amount of fortitude, by one's own immediate family. Invite another crew on board, especially on a bad day when the hatches are battened down against the weather, and in minutes the steam will start to rise, a new and far-from-subtle ambience will develop, and everyone will begin to exchange secret sniffs of disapproval as if Fido had done something tactless on the Axminster.

So far I haven't mentioned the cost of kitting oneself out for sea, mainly because it pains me to do so. Contrary to popular propaganda, sailing is not a cheap recreation. The wind may be free, for the moment anyway, but everything else has its price.

"Then you can wear a big, warm sweater underneath. . .

Your average skipper, having already laid out the kind of money that keeps him awake at nights on his own foul-weather gear, may well suggest that his lady goes for something much lower down the expenditure scale, as befits her subordinate position on board. This is not the time to stand up for your rights. Accept the penny-pinching end of the bargain with alacrity. And when the rain falls, the wind howls, and he says it's your wheel trick, you'll have your ammunition primed and ready to fire.

In fact if you can iron out your demarcation disputes to an ideal level you could well get away with just a light coverall to protect your best silk dress on the row from ship to five-star restaurant ashore. If your natural pessimism prompts you to go for something more sturdy this doesn't rule out up-market eating altogether, but it does mean having to endure the frosty disbelief of an aloof *maître d'hotel* whose offer to "take Madam's . . . er . . . coat" has been answered by a display of grunting and squirming that would give Houdini in sack and chains some stiff competition.

But if we cannot show our full feminine allure while at sea, at least we can comfort ourselves that our menfolk aren't so hot either. Remember that those sexy round-the-world voyagers who set the heart beating faster on TV will have consented to be interviewed only after a shower, a shave and a change of clothes have rendered them acceptable — and probably after the make-up girl has been at them with pan-stick and powder puff to disguise some of the ravages of wind and tide. Even Edward Heath, whom not many of us would place alongside Robert Redford in the swoon-inducing league, can be made to look endearingly cuddly by some well placed lighting, a baby-blue windcheater zipped up to cover an extra chin, and carefully combed silver locks. I bet he doesn't have the same charm coming on watch after three hours' fitful dozing in a pitching bunk on a windswept night.

Or take my skipper. He earns his living as a TV presenter so he's normally the most dapper and well groomed of men, but for

22

sailing he sports the sort of outfit that most tramps would hesitate to wear. The headgear varies, according to mood, from a skimpy bobble hat with a vast bobble — knitted by his mother in an attempt to make up for my wifely deficiencies — to a limp and battered peaked cap that looks as if it first saw service with Casey Jones. His upper portions are encased in a denim smock that has become bleached a pallid grey by ten years of sun and rain and is streaked with a psychedelic design of paint, grease, anti-foul and beer. Beneath it hangs the undulating hem of a hairy and noxious sweater, relinquished for washing only at gunpoint and therefore with a permanent aroma of diesel fumes and old fish.

In an effort to appear at one with the younger set, at the lower end he goes for the ubiquitous blue jeans. Unfortunately the trend away from bell-bottoms seems to have passed him by and for quite a while he walked around with extra yardage flapping in the breeze around ankle level. Eventually he recognised that their ability to ensnare him on deck-fittings was too hazardous, so he hacked them off at mid-calf where they now end in a sort of tatty frill, with trailing strings. He doesn't go in for socks much, maintaining that they're always wet anyway, so next comes an expanse of stark white leg, reminiscent of forced rhubarb, and then the feet. Sometimes these too are left bare and being of the sweaty variety they tend to pick up oil, fluff and dog's hairs — rather off-putting when he puts them up on the table, as he is wont to do when enjoying his end-of-meal coffee. Or he may wear his deck-shoes — items replaced with monotonous regularity but which nevertheless always appear to be on the verge of spontaneous disintegration, with bits of foot showing through in places like some hideous, blanched fungus breaking through a forest floor.

Taken all in all, not a pretty sight.

3

A not-so-magnificent obsession

That the sea can change a man is a well accepted fact. What's not so well known, except to those who have experienced the obsessive behaviour of the average weekend yachtsman, is that he is not the only one to be affected. Children, friends and particularly the woman in his world all find their lifestyle beginning to revolve in new and ever-decreasing circles, with the boat firmly at the centre.

During the summer sailing season, normal social arrangements become virtually impossible. Trying to make a date with friends for a pleasant evening get-together is about as straightforward as planning a Royal Tour, except that Her Majesty is probably slightly more accommodating than your average skipper.

Nor do the winter months bring much relief to the sailing female. The passage-making may be over for another year but now we're into laying-up and then fitting-out time, both of which make tremendous demands on the skipper's leisure hours. It's a forlorn hope that he'll tackle those vital jobs around the home that he promised so glibly to start on 'as soon as the weather turns bad'. The boat, he will remind you, is an investment that needs to be carefully tended if depreciation is not to set in.

If you get your job done at all, it will be a rushed and ham-fisted botch-up, just to keep you quiet while he attends to more

pressing matters down in the boatyard. For months I pressed home to my skipper our urgent need for a small porch over the back door, to prevent half the wet garden being trodden over our expensive carpets each time a child came in. Autumn arrived and suddenly, one weekend, there was a mad flurry of hammering and sawing and a teetering and mis-shapen structure arose in the space of an afternoon. One incautious slam of the door and the whole thing took a ten-degree list to port, the uprights being of split, unseasoned wood and held together only by hastily bashed-in four-inch nails.

"There you are," he said triumphantly at tea-time, with the air of one satisfied by a job well done. "I'll leave you to give it a quick lick of paint, and now don't say I never do anything for you."

With that he disappeared into the potting shed and was gone for a full week. The only evidence of his presence around the place was an occasional sound of sawing, filing and planing, plus the pungent whiff of yacht varnish. At last he emerged from his self-imposed exile clutching with pride a gleaming construction like a leprechaun's loo-seat, highly glossy and ornate, with delicate carved patterning.

"What on earth . . . ?" I began, in some mystification.

"Oh, for heaven's sake," he responded in disgust. "It's a bracket for the oil lamp on 'Mary Lunn'. You kept saying how unstable it was, so I thought I'd give you a nice surprise. I must say, I did expect a bit of gratitude."

The obsession reaches its height when a new boat is in the offing. Once that acquisitive gleam is in his eye, you can forget all about rational behaviour. If you weren't forewarned, you'd think that an adultery petition was pending. At night he'll toss and turn and mutter her name aloud. He may even sneak off at weekends to pay her surreptitious visits. It matters not how much love and care we've put into our present craft during the previous months; let a new lady appear on the scene and suddenly our boat is cast off like an ageing mistress, summarily dismissed as being too small, too cramped and too well worn in comparison to her gleaming rival.

"Oh dear, just look at this," he moans, pointing to almost invisible scars on her topsides, tiny shakes in the locker lids and the cabin light which only works if you thump it. "Poor old girl. She's really had her day, you know."

And although we have, like all regular crews, evolved a system for moving about the boat that avoids too much unwelcome physical contact, suddenly we are always bumping into each other. He goes out of his way to crack his head on the coachroof in an area where we have always boasted full standing headroom.

"It's no good. We've just got to have more space," he cries, reeling dizzily about the saloon.

Such flagrant disloyalty would be forgivable if the boat on offer were the answer to some long-held dream, but my skipper doesn't work that way. He adapts his dream to suit whatever happens to be on the market at the moment he gets the buying urge. Over the years he's claimed, each time with equally cogent reasoning and facts, figures and brochures to support his theories, that the only boat worth sailing was a catamaran, a trimaran, a large monohull, a small monohull, a sleek ocean racer, a sturdy cruiser, a maintenance-free GRP boat, a traditional, handcrafted wooden classic, a motor-sailer and even, in a mad moment, a derelict shrimper with 'great potential'. (To give him his due credit, he was right about that one. We bought her for a song, spent interminable hours — but not a vast amount of money — on lovingly restoring her, and eventually sold her to an enthusiast for a tidy profit. Obsession can occasionally work in one's favour — but only occasionally.)

The affliction is markedly worse at Boat Show times, and unfortunately is not influenced by the state of our bank balance. To hear the skipper chatting up an eager salesman you'd think that money was no object to us anyway. A Greek shipping magnate buying an inflatable runabout would show more regard for the constraints of a limited budget than does my skipper engaging a wily Boat Show salesman in conversation. He's impressed by nothing and pours scorn on everything. Only the hysterical clenching of his besocked toes — shoes removed at the request of the management before boarding — reveals the true level of excitement. The only way to stop him in full flight is for an order form to appear in front of him. Then he, and the commission-prompted glow in the salesman's eye, disappear with remarkable speed.

Many skippers, however, are capable of much more loyalty to their boats and infinitely more self-control. Don't be lulled, though, into thinking that all is well. The boat may be the one you signed your name to, but how about the man? Yesterday's pin-striped insurance clerk can become today's rime-encrusted Ahab at the drop of a shoreline. The mild-mannered become tyrannical and the tough, no-nonsense executives become misty-eyed, far-seeing poets even before the mainsheet has been cleated. You don't even need to be aboard for it to happen. A woman friend assures me that the husband who tenderly hands her into the car at the front gate — "Are you sure the spinnaker isn't in your way, darling?" — degenerates progressively on the drive to the yacht club until by the time they're climbing into the dinghy he's screaming orders in language that would make a Thames-side docker wince.

One change that can be guaranteed, though, is the skipper's attitude to females aboard. No matter how great the responsibilities entrusted to her ashore, a woman on a boat is doomed to being regarded as an incompetent halfwit. It isn't just one's own skipper who piles on this chauvinist pressure. When our boat needed painting, naturally such a mindless and repetitive job fell to me. My skipper occupied himself with more technical matters — in fact he went on a hunt for a bolt of a specific, and apparently rare, type since the task seemed to involve a lot of calling at nearby boats and a great deal of socialising once he got there. I was never alone, though. Each passing skipper, perhaps also engaged in a bolt-hunt, would pause and put in a spell of overseeing and tut-tutting. When my skipper returned, somewhat the worse for wear, they would chat to him across my head, raising their voices above the swishing of my skilful brush.

"I say, old lad," they would bawl, eyeing the shining expanse with envy. "What exactly are you using?"

After the third such enquiry I could stand it no longer and responded, somewhat acidly, "*He* is using *me*, and I am using International Yacht Enamel and a two-inch brush." There was a pause while they digested this outburst and then one of them leaned forward to peer disdainfully at my handiwork.

"And what's more," he drawled, "She's got flies stuck in it."

Some, if not all, of the changes are to the good. At home, for instance, a dinner that offers anything less than red meat and two veg is viewed with shocked disbelief, but at sea my skipper will crow with delight over a mug of instant soup and a crust of three-day-old bread during a night watch. On land, we suffer too from the usual bouts of male hypochondria — a tiny graze is a gash, a slight head cold is potential pneumonia — but in the sailing season it's quite the reverse. In bad weather, his masochistic tendencies come in very handy indeed. With only

"Only £60,000 plus VAT you say?"

narrowed eyes visible above the towelling muffler, he'll keep
her charging on through wind, hail and spray — while at home
he refuses to trail the dog round the block in the face of a mild
drizzle.

It's when you're actually sailing, though, that you'll get the
'skipper syndrome' at its worst. Give him a fine day, enough
wind to make things interesting but not terrifying, and best of
all a visitor to impress, and a skipper is in his element. There he
is at the helm, erect, commanding, ready to demonstrate to all
his mastery of his art, his innate understanding of the ways of
the sea and his skill in crew management. Nothing is ever done

29

to his satisfaction. No sooner do you get the jib sheeted in rock hard than he pauses, sucks in his breath, and orders it eased a foot or two. Then it's "No, not as much as that!" and you have to start all over again while he pours scorn on your lack of muscle power. Make the comment that it might be nice if we all had a break and a snack, and he expresses loud amazement that you can put the needs of your stomach before the needs of the boat. On the other hand, should his mug of cocoa not arrive at what he has privately designated to be the correct moment you'll get dark mutterings about a bit of a cock-up in the galley area.

So you spend a half hour below fighting back queasiness while you boil kettles and throw sandwiches together; you transport the lot on deck — then what happens? He makes an urgent sail change or a wild gybe, that's what. I don't say it's deliberate, but it does stretch the bounds of coincidence a bit far at times. And when everybody has recovered from treading on each other's feet and standing on the ends of the jib sheets, and finished apologising for shoving elbows and backsides in each other's faces, he's got a cockpit plastered with slices of squashed tomato and spilt coffee and a whole new topic to beef about.

But, as most crewpersons will agree, that is as nothing compared to the prima-donna behaviour you get when the task in hand is a trifle trickier. It might be a first approach to an unfamiliar and rock-strewn harbour, or entering a berth in a crowded marina. Your skipper will be fully conscious of his responsibilities, and who can blame him, but he'll also be well aware of the critical scrutiny of his fellows as they view his attempts at seamanship. For although there is a strong camaraderie within the skipper breed, it's still the case that there's nothing they enjoy more than seeing another fool making a lash-up of the job in hand. So, faced with a difficult manoeuvre, your skipper will issue a string of contradictory commands, react with stunned disbelief when you fail to carry them out to the letter, and try to give the impression that he could have done the job, single-handed, in half the time. This serves the dual purpose of both clouding the issue at the time

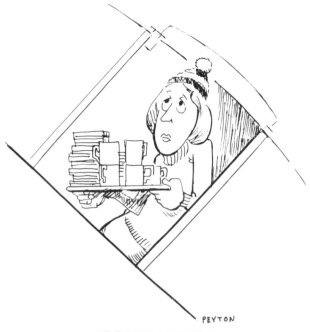

PEYTON

"READY ABOUT!"

and giving him plenty of scope for apportioning blame later on, when he's ensconced in the bar swapping horror stories about crew inadequacies.

I've long since given up any attempt to stop the rot in my own skipper. My main concern these days is to make sure that the laws of heredity are not too closely observed in the future. I stood recently watching with some apprehension as my young son piloted his Mirror dinghy in a series of dramatic swoops amid the moored boats at our anchorage.

"He's really becoming quite skilled," observed a friend, uncannily divining my thoughts, "You're going to have *two* skippers on your boat before long."

I don't think I can stand it.

4

I know where I'm going . . . but I'm not sure how I'll get there

Cruising, even for the most devoted yachtsperson, all too often consists of long periods of unremitting boredom. It's for this reason that I never wear a watch when sailing — I just haven't the willpower not to keep checking it every fifteen minutes (or so I think) only to find that in reality just five have elapsed.

Like many women reared in the tradition that 'a woman's work is never done', long spells of enforced inactivity make me twitchy and frustrated. The only solution seemed to be to take on some vital role in the cruising partnership, something more rewarding than just wondering which tin to open for the next meal. My strong instinct for self-preservation suggested two possibilities — learning to use and maintain the engine, so that if the skipper ever became incapacitated I'd be able to get us all into port without having to do a heroic singlehanded sailing act, and learning navigation, so I'd be able to find a port in the first place.

I will admit I went into the engine idea with a certain amount of distaste because the last thing I wanted was to wind up, as so many ship's mechanics do, looking as if I had a lifetime's membership of the Black Hand Gang. Despite profuse applications of greasy barrier cream, followed by vigorous scrubbing with wire brush and washing-up liquid, I still found that before long my hands, and particularly my previously well manicured fingernails, became filthy with

ingrained oil and dirt, and remained that way for the entire season. For chefs, master bakers and members of the medical profession this could be a severe hazard and even my own skipper has on occasions found his TV career prospects under threat. Watching him engage one of our local politicians in verbal cut-and-thrust recently, viewers may have been disturbed to see what appeared to be a large brown toad, clasping a chocolate éclair, crouched amid the microphones in front of him. To the sailing fraternity, aware of the demands of the fitting-out season, the explanation would have been plain: it was merely his clenched hands with the thumb extended.

I never really did get to grips with the engine proper, although of course I learnt how to start, stop and manoeuvre. As my experience grew I came to realise that no 'Maintenance for Beginners' course, however far-reaching, could truly prepare one for the temperamental and unpredictable behaviour of marine engines in general and ours in particular. I could learn all I liked about cleaning injectors and bleeding the hydraulics or whatever, but that's little help when you've an outboard that likes to leap into the water for a bathe whenever the fancy takes it, or an inboard that coughs, simpers and throws tantrums like a prima donna with first-night nerves. At such times, a frantic skipper belting the infernal contraption with a monkey wrench has just as much chance of success as an evening-class graduate going through the servicing manual step by step.

When we bought the lovely 'Mary Lunn' nobody made any secret of the fact that she was not exactly in peak condition, least of all the vendor, who pointed out with engaging honesty that her engine would need skilled attention and a hefty input of cash before it could be regarded with either confidence or pride. To put it baldly, it had taken a dunking and been left to rust into a solid heap of scrap iron. Mindful of our financial limitations, we did our best. The local expert was called in and after much tongue-clicking gave his verdict: yes, it could be repaired, but at a cost slightly larger than the National Debt. The skipper favoured me with one of his pleading looks, I mentally discarded my notion of a new three-piece suite, and we set off to the suppliers to buy a new one. It might mean beans on toast for a month or two, but peace of mind was worth a few extra bob.

On the first day of our annual cruise we set out light of heart, and when a shackle snapped and our mainsail came thundering down to the deck just a mile or two out we cared little — the wind was virtually non-existent anyway and now our gleaming new engine could show its mettle. At the first touch of the button it leapt into action, with a deep roar of suppressed power. For two more nautical miles it chugged along merrily and then, with a petulant sigh and the faintest of flickers from the oil warning light, expired.

Dumbfounded, we frantically checked everything — the fuel

lines, the tank for diesel, the propeller for rope, and the chart-table locker for the receipt and the warranty card. The Irish coastline grew embarrassingly closer as we grew hotter, dirtier and stickier with the sweat of panic and fury. Fortunately for us, just as it seemed a few well-placed flares were our only hope of salvation, a puff of wind sprang up and we were able to ghost our way into port. Getting back to our marina berth was a little trickier than getting out of it had been but we managed it, and then the fun really started.

Suddenly, everyone who'd ever taken the lid off his own engine and been able to do no more than pour a string of obscenities into its vital parts became an expert on the workings of ours. Conflicting advice flowed in from all sides, although few indeed were the brave souls prepared to put their spanners where their mouths were. So I held the torch while the skipper scrabbled around, and he held the torch while I delved into the bilges for the parts he'd dropped, then he cranked her over while I threw levers and vice versa, and nothing we did made the slightest difference. We engaged in lengthy and expensive mutual recriminations over the telephone with the suppliers of this mutinous machine, and did our best to carry out their instructions. So it went on, with each day bringing some fresh frustration, until at last we'd had enough. One bright morning we rigged up our own lifting tackle from a child's garden swing, a network of ropes and pulley, all the musclepower we could gather from nearby boats, and the strength born of sheer exasperation, and hauled out the whole thing and shipped it, with a terse note expressing our disgust, back home to roost.

We never did find out, officially, what had caused the loss of an entire cruising season for us, but many weeks later the skipper on a progress check with the suppliers which had now become a regular part of the weekly routine, did point out a large piece of decayed gasket which was floating in the exposed oil-delivery pipe and was told, with every evidence of relief on their part, that yes, that could have been at the root of the trouble. Suffice it to say that shortly after this revelation, we received a replacement engine and I, once and for all, abandoned any idea of becoming ship's engineer.

On the navigation front I fared quite a bit better. The skipper fully approved of this move because we both felt that although our navigation thus far had been effective — in that we'd managed to get from place to place without wrecking ourselves or anybody else — it had also probably relied rather too heavily on luck as opposed to sound judgement and a thorough knowledge of the subject. And since one of us would have to undergo specialised training we were also in accord that I was the most suitable candidate. When it comes to matters mathematical, the skipper's credentials aren't exactly impressive. He began failing his school exams shortly after the class progressed beyond 'twice times' and the teacher took away his counting frame. Ask him for a reciprocal bearing and all you get is a blank stare, plus some nervous shifting of the eyes.

So when the evening class started up in our area he was only too pleased to pack me off, clutching pencil, rubber, dividers and parallel rules, to be taught my trade. However, things didn't kick off to an auspicious start. As I poked my head around the door of the appointed lecture room it was apparent that I had taken both the instructor and my classmates — all male — by surprise. Female emancipation had plainly been slow in reaching the navigational end of the Further Education Institute. "No, dear, Flower Arranging is two doors down or Hostess Cookery, third on your left," said the instructor with a bright smile which might be described, if one were sensitive about such matters, as supremely patronising. Rejecting the idea of coming over the female militant there and then, on the grounds that there was no point in increasing hostility, I instead opted for the 'fragile little woman' technique (no mean skill when you stand almost six foot in your socks).

"Actually," I simpered, with a blush of sugary innocence, "I was looking for Coastal Navigation? I wonder if you could

Navigation is not an exact science.

possibly point me in the right direction?" It was a hit. Following the instructor's lead, they fell about in their seats.

"Oh well," he wheezed, wiping a tear of mirth from his eye. "If you can't even find the classroom on your own then I reckon you do need help."

After that he, and my new classmates, gathered me to their collective bosom like nursery school teachers parting a reluctant three-year-old from its mother's apron strings. Unfortunately, the similarity didn't end there. While the instructor, understandably enough, treated the whole class as rank beginners, *I* was treated as a backward infant. After a while I couldn't help finding it a trifle irksome that while the men were informed once of the workings of the parallel rules, I was told three times, very slowly and clearly, and given a personal demonstration to boot.

"You see, Lesley? They can walk right across the map. Only we call it a 'chart', don't we?"

OK, so maybe I wasn't the most brilliant pupil in the room but it wasn't me who complained loudly that a chart was faulty and then discovered that the compass rose was on the bit folded underneath, nor was it me who asserted that our allowance for leeway and tide took us straight into the Mountains of Mourne. *I* didn't stretch my dividers until they were doing the splits and then wonder whether I should have bought a longer pair. But, funnily enough, it *was* always me that got the desk top with the screw heads sticking out, so that my walks with the parallels persistently came to abrupt halts and my rhumb lines looked more like markings for severe overfalls. And it was always *my* table that would suddenly erupt into violent motion at a crucial moment and I'd look up, with murder in my heart, to find the instructor gaily swinging on the end of it.

"Oh yes, it's all very easy in a nice warm classroom," he'd snigger, "But this is what it'll be like doing chartwork when you're at sea!"

And because, unlike most of my classmates, I'd already put in some passage-making, my charts were held up to ridicule and scorn.

"Just look at this!" he'd cry in mock horror, waving a chart decorated with soup stains, cocked hats allowing margins for error of several nautical miles, little doodles of mermaids and sharks' fins, and rubbings out which had failed to erase the running fixes but had removed large portions of coastline. "How can she expect a correct result if she's not working on a clean chart?"

Now it just so happens that since those early days I've met some experienced and far-travelled yachtsmen, and I've seen their charts. Charts which look as if they've been used for some first attempts at origami; charts that have been folded incorrectly so many times that the heaviest crewman has to sit on them before they can be stowed; charts which have been ripped apart during the course of some navigational dispute and later been joined together, slightly askew, with sticky tape; charts that have had so many dunkings and rapid dryings that they look like a large helping of flaky pastry. But a clean chart, never. So why make a big deal out of mine? For the woman who wants to navigate, dogged determination and a brass neck are essential features, it seems.

Certainly it must have been something of the sort that kept me turning up regularly week after week, because my initial enthusiasm soon began to flag. Long before we got to the lecture on cloud formations, which was so boring that we took it in turns to fall asleep across the projector and block out his slides of cirro-stratus, I'd ceased to care if the sky fell on me. I didn't even have the energy to join in the recriminations when he'd set us an impossible task, due to a gross error on his part, let us all struggle for an hour, and then leaped up to the blackboard with all the brilliance of hindsight and cry, "Now then, did anyone spot my deliberate mistake?" Just try handing that line to a skipper stranded on a sandbank and see how far it gets you.

In spite of all this I did manage to pick up some knowledge somewhere along the way, and found it added enormously both to my confidence and my pleasure when sailing. For at least part of the time it meant that the boat was being sailed under my directions, and because navigation is not an exact science, there are always a string of ready-made excuses if things go wrong — a freak tide, a magnetic anomaly, the incompetence of the helmsman and so on. With sufficient ingenuity and quick thinking, the navigator can always have the last word.

And that's something every woman enjoys.

5

Galley slave

Even in these days of working wives, househusbands and shared responsibility in most things, it's a reasonable bet that the female aboard a boat will have to spend a fair proportion of her time in the galley. It's an even better bet that she'll have to spend an *unfair* portion of her time there. Indeed if she doesn't scream, shout and froth at the mouth a bit she'll no doubt find that she's been handed the entire operation of shopping, cooking, serving out and washing up afterwards.

Even having obtained a theoretical agreement that it's her holiday too and that a break from dull routine would be nice, getting it put into practice is yet another matter to be fought over. My skipper will insist loudly and often, both to me and the children, that crewing a boat means lending a hand with *all* aspects of the cruise. He has at times drawn up complicated duty rosters, with a system of 'no work no pocket money' enforcement for the kids, but these have always proved themselves unworkable, usually by the end of the first day, and have to be remodelled or abandoned due to unforeseen extenuating circumstances. For example, since Mum has the best knowledge of shops, prices and foodstuffs it might be more sensible to leave the stocking up — and so all the fetching, carrying and stowage — to her, while the rest of the crew get on with last-minute preparations on board. For some reason these seem to entail the consumption of large quantities of bottled

beer and a great deal of loafing around on bunks reading yachting magazines. Glancing up from his pleasure couch the skipper may catch a glimpse of my exploratory foot as it feels its way past the porthole groping for a secure spot to land, since I can't see anything over a cardboard box piled high with assorted groceries. Pricked by a guilty conscience, or perhaps concerned about a large chunk of the holiday cash winding up on the bottom if I slip, he leaps to my aid.

"Good heavens, woman," he cries, somehow making me the

culprit. "Didn't I tell you I'd give you a hand with all that stuff? I don't see why you always have to make a martyr of yourself."

Nevertheless, he does understand how we women feel about galley chores and he promises that, once we're away, he'll take his turn at the spud-bashing and porridge stirring. *But* just on the first leg, while he irons out a few problems on deck, it might be as well if I have some ready-prepared meals on hand. Quite right too, of course, but unfortunately ready-made meals also make ready-made washing-up. Not to worry, just stow it in the sink and he'll take care of it when we hit port. Funny thing though; when we do reach port he immediately has to have a brief chat with the harbourmaster — who just happens to be in the pub; or he has to take the dog ashore to do what cruising doggies must — with difficulty when tied up to a bench outside the pub; or he needs to get water cans refilled — from a tap at the back of the pub. You get the picture, I trust. Much later on he returns, in jovial mood, to find the washing-up done, the galley immaculate and me, sullen, resentful and ready for a full, frank exchange of views.

So, overcome with remorse, he volunteers to do the big thing the following morning and make breakfast. This is an idle whim, induced by the consumption of large quantities of bottled *bonhomie*, and I dismiss it as such. However, the next day, his slumbers having been curtailed by the call of nature, he remembers his rash words. I have been snoring peacefully, dreaming of safe marinas and eccentric millionaires who've taken a fancy to me, when suddenly I'm jolted awake by a high-pitched wail that throws back my eyelids like snack-bar shutters at opening time. We seem to be on fire. Emerging from my sleeping bag at a run, I find the whistling kettle about to go into orbit while half my week's stock of bacon turns into charred ruins in the pan. Of the skipper, there is no trace. I snap off the gas and dash up on deck, clad in little but a furious snarl, brandishing the smoking remains of breakfast. I find the skipper, gently nursing his early morning cuppa, leaning dreamily against the mast, lost in the beauty of the nautical

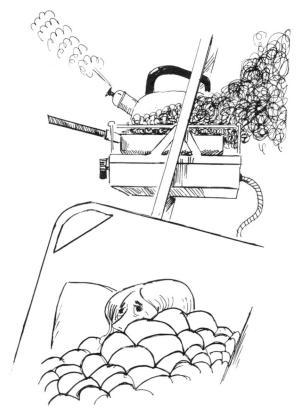

"I had a little surprise planned for you . . ."

world coming to life around him.

"Oooh," he wails in hypocritical disappointment. "What are *you* doing awake? I had a little surprise planned for you." I inform him, acid dripping from my voice along with the bacon fat falling onto his precious teak decking, that I've had the surprise and have not been unduly bowled over by it. I explain, as explicitly as my command of language allows, just what is the inevitable result of leaving a whistling kettle, a

43

superheated frying pan, and a sleeping wife to their own devices for extended periods. Once again, he's all abject contrition.

"Never mind, sweetheart, just you pop back into your bunk and I'll bring you breakfast in bed to make up for it," he offers sweetly.

Determined to make his point, he will brook no arguments at this stage, so back I go. It's not long before the mutterings (intended of course for my ears) start: "Where the hell's the marmalade? How are you supposed to keep bacon hot while you cook the eggs? Damn it, that's three yolks broken now. How do you scramble the darned things anyway? Oh God, there goes the toast again! How am I supposed to set up the table when she's sleeping on it?"

But I'm pretty determined too, so I lie on in the face of it all, despite the tension stiffening my every limb, until we reach the climax of the performance. This takes the form of a plaintive yelp of agony, half-heartedly stifled, and a wild dance around the saloon with much flapping of hands.

"Now what have you done?" I demand, with grim resignation. "Oh nothing, nothing at all," he responds through gritted teeth. "Don't give it a thought. It was just a small gush of boiling coffee and I don't use my left hand all that much anyway. If you could just give me a few clues as to where you've hidden the first-aid kit I'm sure I'll survive."

But I know when I'm beaten. It still galls me, though, that once having eaten a passable re-make of his burnt offerings he'll lie back, belch with satisfaction, and then say to the kids, "Now I just hope you'll both follow my example and show Mummy some consideration in future. She does need a little looking after, you know."

In the end, all this much-vaunted break from routine means is that I get the chance to do all the things I'd do at home, only in the most trying of circumstances, such as while plunging into a head sea with the floor where the walls should be.

"I really don't know how you do it!" cry my shore-based

sisters, viewing my gimballed cooker with horror. I wonder myself. Certainly the designers have done their best to establish a bit of order about the place but sometime it's the very nitpicking nature of their plans which defeats the nautical cook. "Compact galley area, designed to maximise every inch of stowage!" the brochure trumpets. How right. A six-berth cruiser has neat little stowage holes for six of everything, which is grand if you happen to be equally methodical by temperament. But if you're like me and throw in a little bit extra for luck and slap-happy dishwashing, you always have too many vital items for too few storage spaces. These then have to be stowed on the 'bung it in and slam the door quickly' principle, which works well until you want something. Needing a plate in a hurry to jam under a red-hot egg you find either they've wedged together so tightly that none will emerge, or else you get the whole lot at once, hurtling across the saloon like a volley of multicoloured Frisbees.

Not all of us are lucky enough to boast modern, intricately designed yachts anyway — our 'Mary Lunn' is an elderly wooden lady, built in Bombay around forty years ago. Although she's thirty-six feet over-all her interior appears to have been designed for two occupants only, who sailed in one set of clothes and ate all their meals ashore. We do have a marble washbasin and brass taps that would dwarf a village pump, but locker space consists of a couple of dark cupboards so deep and inaccessible you'd need a trained ferret to get out the contents.

The nerve-centre for the sailing cook is of course the cooker itself. Types of stoves vary and each has its own disadvantages. Paraffin or meths stoves, which offer more versatility and have safety advantages over their bottled-gas rivals, nevertheless take a lot of getting to know and a steady nerve on the part of the lighter-upper. While one look at the results of a gas explosion may be enough to turn some of us into cold-meat-and-salad devotees for life, one must still weigh up the pro's and cons of paraffin against gas. Which is the more off-putting: the chance, a rare one but nonetheless real for that, of a nasty and destructive bang as your gas bottle goes, or the day-to-day possibility of greeting the world without eyebrows and with a suddenly receded hairline because you were caught in an unexpected blast of sooty paraffin flame?

Having made several mad dashes from the saloon with a fiercely burning Tilley lamp, the skipper and I have always opted for the turn-of-the-tap convenience of gas for cooking. But being both cautious and cowardly by nature we're ever mindful of its potential for disaster. We each spend a lot of time sniffing around the cooker and the bottle-locker on deck like bloodhounds after the murder weapon, but it's hard to spot a gas leak in this way. The snag is that so many shipboard activities — varnishing, refuelling the tanks, cooking tinned curry, or forgetting to flush the heads — provide a plethora of mystifying pongs which can give you quite the wrong impression. Let one of us wake in the morning feeling thick-headed and queasy and we're immediately rubbing soap solution over the pipes and swearing we can see bubbles forming, even though we might more justifiably attribute the furry tongue and the sludgy brain to the half-bottle of Scotch consumed the previous evening. I'd hate to have a serious gas leak for more than safety reasons, though: I'm told that the gas seeps down into the bilges and has to be baled out in invisible bucketfuls, and chucked over the side. Sound sense I'm sure, but you'd feel such an idiot, wouldn't you?

When it comes to fitting out the galley with equipment, as little as possible and of the highest quality possible is the golden rule. Like many other sea-going couples we began our nautical career suffering under slight cash-flow problems so pots, pans and eating irons had to be strictly of the low-cost economy type. Now that we're older and wiser, although not noticeably better off financially, we've learnt that it's no saving in the long run to buy cheap stuff for rough use. Now our family home is equipped with bent and blackened cheapies and the boat has the pricey, heavy-based non-stick jobs. This makes

Grab-a-quick-bite-while-we've-got-the-chance

washing up a simpler task which in the absence of hot water can still be performed with some success using only crumpled-up toilet roll. We can even indulge in such previously forbidden delicacies as scrambled egg, porridge, semolina pudding and tomato soup, without having to cook the next meal on top of the carbonised remnants of the previous one. Likewise by investing in good-quality cutlery we've got rid of the mediaeval banquet syndrome of tearing our meat apart with bare hands when our cheap knives and forks had snapped off at the handles. And since the majority of our on-passage meals are cooked in the rushed, grab-a-quick-bite-while-we've-got-the-chance manner that unpredictable weather demands, tough meat is a regular feature of our cuisine.

The most useful item in any sailing chef's armoury, apart from the corkscrew of course, is that good old reliable, the frying pan. I've read all that the healthy-living experts have to say about animal fats and high levels of cholesterol and I don't doubt their wisdom but I still couldn't get by without my faithful friend. It works quickly and efficiently, fills the air with mouthwatering aromas and even sounds busy and happy in its work. I like a great big one, with high sides and lid handy to minimise the splattering and I find it's the most versatile tool of the lot. I can fry in it, grill in it, boil up soups and stews in it. I can use it for pancakes, drop scones and I've even unscrewed the handle and baked a passable chocolate cake in it when the mood for celebration overtook us. When we're feeling really slovenly, we can plonk it in the middle of the table and let the whole family eat from it without the need to dirty plates, and it also comes in handy for breaking up ice-blocks for the cool-box, stunning fresh-caught mackerel, threatening rebellious children with physical violence or using as an emergency bailer for the dinghy. It's a measure of the high regard I have for my trusty fryer that when any other piece of gear has been carelessly lost to the deeps I've shrugged it off with only a mild reprimand for the culprit, but when the skipper dropped in the frying pan I made him dive till he retrieved it.

What foodstuffs one chooses to take along on a cruise must depend to some extent on what exactly one's family will eat but I do think that two important factors should be borne in mind. First, if they're hungry enough they'll eat almost anything, however finicky they may be at home, and secondly, some of the most popular foodstuffs are frankly rather unsuitable for the cruising galley. Take the humble egg, for instance. In almost any sailing epic you care to read you'll find a description of the back-up team spending days on end dipping eggs into candlewax or isinglass or whatever it is they use as a preservative these days; and I dare say a supply of natural protein is important when you plan to be out of sight of land for months on end. Personally I've never quite managed to come to terms with the egg as a cruising companion. Their versatility I won't deny — they can make thorough nuisances of themselves in all sorts of ways. Stow them too long and they go bad with a pong like the skipper's wellies on a warm day. Stow them incautiously and they shatter so you get a cool-locker that looks as though a giant slug had run amok inside.

And what can you do anyway with an egg in a lumpy sea? Make an omelette? Have you tried to control an omelette on a bouncing plate? Boil them? Who carries egg-cups on a boat? I don't because I refuse valuable locker space to any item that does not have at least two uses and egg-cups have yet to prove themselves as bailers, slop buckets or even for serving the occasional dry martini. Scramble them? It's easy enough to achieve — the eggs do it for you — but as for serving, see omelettes, above. Fry them? Despite my earlier treatise on the virtues of the frying pan, it's strictly for in-port use in my book; otherwise you'll fry your fingers in hot fat as the pan swings up to meet you, and at best you'll get eggs that all hurtle together to one side of the pan and lie there, piled inseparably on top of each other, gazing up at you in sullen, yellow-eyed resentment. When I feel like an egg — and you can keep the funny remarks to yourself, thank you — I buy them fresh, in port (even in the remotest ports you can usually find a cooperative farmer or, more to the point, a cooperative hen) and scoff the lot before setting sail again.

Other items which the experts seem to regard as essential to a healthy sailor's diet are fresh meat, fish, green vegetables and lots of citrus fruit. Again I can imagine that this would be the required fare when there was a real possibility of scurvy or rickets developing, but for your average leisure sailors, and more particularly for their children who spend the winter months being crammed with large doses of expensive vitamins, something less will probably suffice for the short spell of a holiday. Fresh fish is, of course, a money-saving feature of the diet if you have a keen angler on board, and if you discount the initial cost of rods, reels, and a collection of 'fool-proof' lures which regularly get lost in weed, or as the angler will have it "bitten clean off by something really big". However, while the fishing may be fun, the cleaning, gutting, and hosing down the boat afterwards aren't all that appealing to the cook.

Unless you have the kind of boat that boasts a deep-freeze you're going to have to put up with convenience foods for at least part of the time anyway, so why not go the whole hog, give the cook a break, and have as many ready-prepared, canned, dehydrated, and otherwise labour-saving meals as possible? The only concession to culinary expertise which I make when boating is to bring along a small selection of herbs and spices.

Needless to say, cookery books have no place in a well-run galley where improvisation is the essence of the chef's art. Thus we get such rare delicacies as 'Chilli con Corned-Beef', 'Instant Potato Bolognese', and 'Shipping Forecast Pie', which is similar to Shepherd's Pie but has less predictable contents. I rarely pass on recipes, mainly because afterwards I can never remember just how I threw together any menu that had particular appeal. However, here is a typical snippet from the Black book of 'boat cuisine' which has made many a lone night watch slightly more endurable. I could give it a fancy title, such as 'Pain à la Bretonaise' perhaps, but it's known to my lot as 'Hot Onion Sog' and that's good enough for me. Make it as follows:

1 Check setting on autopilot. Check horizon for bulk tankers, schools of killer whales, etc.
2 Nip below, fill kettle and put on to boil.
3 Dash back on deck for several large gasps of fresh air.
4 Become aware of kettle screaming. Repeat step 1.
5 Half fill mug with dehydrated onion. Pour on boiling water. Leave to swell.
6 Repeat step 3.
7 Slap butter, marge or any other waterproof layer onto two slices close-weave bread and add a blob of Marmite. Scoop out handful of hot swollen-up onion. Swear liberally at scalded fingers. Drop onion on one slice, top with the other and squash vigorously to seal. Top up oniony mug with hot water, stir in more Marmite.
8 Repeat step 3, carrying meal with you and consume same, adding rain and sea-water to taste.

Eat your heart out, Fanny Cradock!

6

From the cradle to the wave

A 'happy event', to the nautical breed, does not *always* refer to the delivery of a new boat. Though one could sometimes think otherwise, outside the sailing scene the world does go on, and new life has a habit of appearing and making its needs and demands plainly felt. Once skipper and mate have combined to produce a tiny new crew-member they rapidly discover that sailing with children aboard, without incurring mutiny or infanticide, is an art all by itself. And inevitably, it's the woman aboard who has to bear the brunt of it.

It doesn't matter how much you promise yourself that *they* will have to learn to fit in with *your* way of life, that they'll soon settle down happily to nautical routines, nor how many dreams you cherish of a healthy, liberated family laughing with joy as they guide their immaculate cruising home into a glowing sunset — sooner or later the truth will dawn. Kids on board boats get in your way, under your skin, and generally work their insidious wiles to such an extent that their presence dominates each waking hour, and probably quite a few sleeping ones too.

There is no demanding passage, perhaps a dirty beat into a foul tide on a grey and drizzling day, that can't be made even worse by the addition of a number of lively young minds with too much to say and not enough to do. There is no fiddly shipboard task, perhaps the intricate repair of some virtually

51

unreachable part of the ship's engine that requires extreme delicacy of touch and breath-stopping accuracy, that can't be rendered even more irritating by a little woolly head persistently blocking all available light, tiny probing fingers anxious to point out all the bits you've dropped into the bilge-water, and that strident young voice posing the perennial question, "What are you *trying* to do, Daddy?" Even a peaceful night at anchor in a quiet moonlit bay can be ruined by the wearisome yo-yoing from sleeping bag to fo'c'sle in answer to pathetic little cries of distress, "Mummy, I need a drink/a biscuit/a pee/a story. . ." or, oh joy of joys, "my bunk keeps going up and down and I think I'm going to be sick."

You could of course leave them behind, but that presupposes two highly unlikely factors — one, that you've kids sufficiently well trained to accept being farmed out regularly while you go swanning off to have fun, and two, that you have plenty of equally accommodating friends and relatives to take them.

No, the truth is that the younger you start the acclimatisation process, the better it will be for all concerned and if that means nappies flapping at the yardarm and feeding bottles taking the place of gin bottles in the drinks locker, so be it. Our two youngsters saw their first nautical miles over the rim of their carrycots, and while it made a lot of extra work it was fun and had the added bonus that the children accepted the sailing way of life as the norm when they were still too young to raise any objections.

There were other advantages too. The motion of the seas does induce the infant to sleep for a great deal of the day — which can be a tremendous relief to the parents of the fractious brat who at home inexplicably bawls from dawn till dusk. If the movement becomes extreme, however, the soporific effect can be dramatically reversed. Babies are sadly ill-equipped for balancing themselves against force 6-plus conditions and find themselves catapulted around their cradles like peas in a whistle. If the cot itself is not firmly anchored into place, they may be treated to a helter-skelter ride across the vinyl with

each dip and roll of the boat. We beat this one by investing in tiny hammocks — not the string variety, as little arms and legs fall through the holes and get bent in unnatural and painful directions, but good stout canvas. If it was good enough for the Royal Navy it was good enough for us, and we sailed many miles with our gimballed babies contentedly snoring below decks.

The major nuisance of running a nautical crèche is the feeding process. Not only the bunging in of grub at the top end at frequent intervals — although that calls for a strong nerve and a steady hand if the saloon is not to be liberally daubed with strained prunes — but also the results produced at the less pleasant end of the infant.

Fabric nappies, requiring soaking, washing and drying, are nonstarters. My stomach rebels long before I get the scraping bit over and anyway the skipper takes a dim view of sailing a boat that looks like a travelling laundry. And once the steering jammed as we were bearing down on harbour traffic and he went berserk when he discovered that the cause of the upset was a tight wodge of nappies that I'd secreted on the steering lines running through the aft lockers.

Hurray, therefore, for paper nappies. Unfortunately they do

take a little time to sink to the abodes of crab and lugworm so it is a somewhat antisocial gesture to lob them overboard in a crowded anchorage, to drift back and forth on the tide like an invasion of insanitary jellyfish. Storing for later disposal leads to a saloon with an interesting ambience and continued visitations from the local bluebottle population.

When our children were at this stage we owned a Fairey Atalanta which had holes in the cockpit sole housing our retractable keels — very handy for posting used nappies into the deep unseen. When we upped anchor we did leave our own little pool of pollution behind, but by the time this became apparent to nearby crews, we were long gone.

The toddler period brought a whole new set of potential disasters. Now wanderlust had set in and no locker was safe. Gas taps could be turned, stopcocks opened, cans of diesel or meths unscrewed and the contents sampled or spilled. Eternal vigilance became our lot. Off watch on the helm meant on watch with the kids, and though night passaging was easier there was fat chance of rest in the daylight hours. Even in port it was hard to relax. It's truly staggering just how many times per hour a small child can hopelessly entangle even a short lifeline, while lifejackets for this age group are so bulky in proportion to the kid's height that it's small wonder they become bundles of impotent frustration wearing one for any length of time.

Naturally I've kept my eyes open to see how other parents manage, but I've yet to see anything other than constant watchfulness as a solution. I've seen toddlers left to wander the cockpit freely on the assumption that it forms an adequate playpen, and I've also seen the frantic grabs to haul them back when they surprised everybody by doing a quick ascent of the ship's wheel preparatory to diving into the blue. I've seen boats with the guardrails raised and filled in with strong mesh — works a treat, if you don't mind sailing a craft that looks like a municipal tennis court. I've seen one babe strapped into a car-seat and hooked onto the gunwales — downright dangerous,

Mona was here!!!

this one, as car-seats and the babies strapped to them are not designed to float should they get an accidental knock.

Somehow they eventually grow to the stage when they can think for themselves and perhaps even appreciate the reasons for the safety precautions. Life should get easier then, but not a bit of it. The next problem is boredom, especially if they're still too small to take an active part in the sailing.

You can bet your wellies that the little dears will show no interest whatsoever in all the toys they insisted were indispensible when packing. Their selection of vital recreational equipment produces much acrimonious argument in our house, and is resolved only by a system of sabotage and bribery. I remove the bulkier items on the sly, and if I'm caught pacify them with wild promises of pocket money yet to come. This solution did cause a nasty period of incipient mutiny when we went to the Outer Hebrides and they discovered that toyshops were thinner on the ground than they'd been led to believe. Still, they bought up half of Woolworths when we reached Stornoway and honour was restored.

In the meantime, they amuse themselves by misusing the ship's equipment. You reach for a shackle in a hurry and find you've got a dozen or so linked up like a complex model of a

DNA molecule. You grab a handy warp and find it's converted to a giant cat's cradle, or it has been made into a hangman's noose and Teddy is gasping his last while swinging from the boom. The nuts-and-bolts box is usually empty, the contents having been dumped into the bilges so the children can fish for them with a magnet. (The expensive stainless steel ones of course stay put and an irate skipper has to grovel for them later.) Their favourite sport, however, is fender trailing — letting a fender out on a long line astern and watching it ride the wake. We personalise them by giving names and faces. At first we used 'permanent' marker for the artwork but it failed to live up to its name and neighbouring crews looked askance at the imprints left on their topsides when we tied up, so now we steal the skipper's insulating tape for the job, and lay bets as to whose features will stay put the longest.

Fear is another problem that children bring into sharp focus. On our boat it's usually *my* fear that they underline, either by joining in my tearful gibbering when I give way to panic, or by constantly needling me to talk or play Scrabble when I'm trying to put fear at bay with a little white-faced, tight-lipped silence. I know all about the theory that adults should be pillars of solid calm and comfort in times of stress, and I'm sure it's right. I'm just not very good at it, that's all.

When I do offer reassurances they are not necessarily accepted anyway. The young mind can see with devasting clarity through adult evasions and false jollity. It takes only a couple of rides through 'just this funny little bumpy bit up ahead' for them to sigh with grim resignation and reach for the bucket the next time they hear the announcement. Fortunately seasickness doesn't seem to bother kids too much. Throw up and shut up is their motto.

Making a crossing of the Irish Sea not so long ago we tried, unsuccessfully, to outrun a bad forecast and strayed into the outer limits of the tide-rip off the Mull of Kintyre. Reefed to almost nothing, we made slow progress as we surged and wallowed in heavy seas. The grey skies of a wet dawn did little

to lighten the gloom and then, above the noise of wind and wave, we heard sad little cries from below. Grabbing a couple of buckets I went to administer what comfort I could, but was able only to wedge myself into position between their bunks and try to keep the two receptacles in roughly the right place. There followed an unpleasant time during when they zealously filled the buckets — and the pocket on the front of my oilies. I began to get worried, knowing we had nine hours still to go at best, but all was well. With a final heave, both sighed with apparent satisfaction, bade me good morning, snuggled back into their now somewhat fragrant sleeping bags and we heard no more from them. Not that is until we'd safely tied up in port and the skipper and I were pouring ourselves a couple of very stiff Scotch malts to restore shattered nerves. Two sleepy heads reappeared, took in the situation at a glance, and demanded to be taken ashore for a fish supper and ice cream.

But, if we find sailing with kids something of a trial, I can't help wondering what it makes them think about us. Do they swap horror stories about our irrational behaviour as we do about theirs?

I wondered about this after an unhappy incident that occurred as we were running down the Sound of Mull before a stiff breeze. We kept receiving whingeing complaints from the senior offspring about funny noises coming from below his bunk. It was my trick on the wheel so the skipper took on the parental responsibility of understanding and reassurance, and I heard him telling the child, in loving tones, to belt up and go back to sleep. Scarcely had the words left his lips when there was a loud bang, from below that very bunk, which flushed him out like a startled owl and the steering line parted leaving the wheel spinning impotently in my hands. I prefer not to dwell too much on the next few moments — the dust in the mouth, the jelly in the knees, the ferry to the Isles closing fast, while the skipper frantically lashed a jury tiller to the rudder stock. We limped into the first available shelter, badly shaken. As it happened we fetched up alongside a boat whose crew we'd befriended earlier on. One of their kids yelled a greeting to our son up on deck.

"Hello", we heard him bawl. "Ask if you can come for a row in our dinghy. Where's your mum?"

"Oh, she's sitting on her bunk", announced our son with the air of one who was accustomed to such things. "She's crying and drinking gin."

What a splendid picture of maternal devotion for him to carry with him into his adult years.

7

Laughing fellow rovers

One of the ploys sometimes used by keen skippers to encourage a reluctant mate to get involved in sailing is the 'Do come along, you'll enjoy the company' line. The yachting scene, they'd have you believe, is a nonstop round of backslapping joviality and camaraderie where everybody is ever willing to lend a hand to help others. Don't be fooled.

The scene is a popular yacht harbour as evening draws in. The experienced skippers are all tied up at jealously guarded berths and, having exchanged initial pleasantries, are now engaged in dismantling part of the engine or studying the passing scene — both of which are cover-up activities so they can eavesdrop on the conversations held in deafening whispers on the boats next door.

"I've told you, if I'm spoken to like that once more I'm taking the next train home," hisses an aggrieved wife. "And you can stop lounging on that bunk and peel the potatoes — I'm not here to be anybody's drudge, let me tell you!"

Suddenly there appears a latecomer with a novice crew — easily identifiable by a skipper yelling orders in a highpitched squeal just short of hysteria, a deckhand doing battle with a viciously flailing mainsail, and a wild-eyed wife, bow-warp gripped in her teeth, struggling to bring down the jib without first freeing the halyard. The skipper is hauling on the tiller as if it were some kind of hydraulic braking system while his gaze swings along the assembled craft, seeking a welcome and finding none. "Permission to come alongside?" he yells desperately to the empty air as the skippers disappear below like rabbits facing a round of buckshot. His final throes won't go unobserved, though, as a battery of hostile eyes, family quarrels forgotten, appear at the portholes and the crash of his uprooted stanchions is all but drowned by a chorus of clicking tongues and exaggerated moans of disbelief. So much for the 'laughing fellow rovers' theory.

Even when you make an effort to extend the hand of friendship, you can't be sure it will be warmly clasped. I remember once heading into a small Scottish loch in search of shelter as several other boats did the same. In the very best spot, on a mooring buoy, was one of those floating gin palaces — the kind that has a speed-boat slung on davits and electric table lamps with suede shades illuminating the smoked salmon on the dining table. Sipping their martinis, with a snazzy striped awning to keep off the driving rain, were the owner and his lady. As each of us passed, miserably handing out anchor chain and spitting out stray bits of wet hair, they would raise their glasses and give that hearty greeting so much favoured by the ruling classes, "Bit of a blow, what? Haw, haw, haw." And each of us, I report with some shame, kept our heads down and pretended we hadn't heard a single guffaw. Not so the crew of the boat which came thundering in just as night was falling. It was a small, well used craft, manned by about twenty huge and hairy Scots who had plainly been having a rough ride and were in no mood for pleasantries. They made straight for the gin palace, and the owner, sensing a possible conquest, once again leapt to his feet with a cry of glee.

"Rough night, old boy, eh? Glad to get in, I'll be bound. Ha, ha!"

The new arrival fixed him with a frosty eye, utterly devoid of humour.

"Ay," he breathed with menace, "And ye're on me mooring. I'll thank ye to shift yersel' and dae it noo!" For the rest of us,

"Ay — and ye're on me mooring."

the next half hour of revving and shunting was pure joy. We're a nasty lot, at heart.

In fact there's almost nothing a crew enjoys more than seeing some other poor sucker making a mess of things — we don't wish them serious harm, of course, just some temporary and (for us) highly diverting embarrassment. Around the Irish waters which are my own home ground, such incidents tend to happen quite frequently.

In a local harbour, for instance, there's a spot at the head of the pier which is plainly stated in the pilot to be a foul berth — and it's foul because the pierhead toilets have an outlet in the wall which, at low water, is about 4 feet above deck level. Visiting boats, quite often from the continent, seem unaware of this minor health hazard and tie up there happily, congratulating themselves on getting a berth so close to all amenities; and so far I've never seen a friendly local put them right. On one occasion, we saw a bronzed Gallic matelot, resplendent in pure white shoregoing gear, decide to display his athleticism to the local female talent by going hand over hand up a shoreline, past the offending pipe. And what did we do? We all just held our breath and waited to see if a flush would sound at precisely the right moment — and it did. With hypocritical cries of sympathy we turned to catch each other's rolled eyes and snigger in foxy conspiracy.

Not everybody deserves such callous treatment from his fellows, and it's never wise to shout too loudly anyway: you may be next, and if you're a woman it's as well to bear in mind that if your boat should be the one to blunder it's a pound to a penny that the blame will somehow wind up at your door.

Some skippers, however, simply ask for it. Personally, I've a deep loathing for those who make great play of the early-morning, bright-and-breezy bit — as if it were some praiseworthy achievement to be up with the lark. We met a bloke in a pub one night — the skipper of a famous ocean racer, which shall be nameless — who went on and on about how he'd whipped his crew into line and how, while we were all still

Going up hand over hand past the offending pipe.

grunting in our fusty sleeping bags with hangovers, *he* would be up, up and away putting up record times on the bounding main. Worse still, he proved his words were not mere hollow boasting by leaving at half-past four the next morning with as much noise — in the form of bellowed and totally unnecessary commands — as possible. "Stand by the starboard fenders!" (at 0430 hours? In a sleeping harbour?)

Small wonder, then, that those of us who dragged ourselves topside to wish him gone enjoyed a moment of unholy anticipation when we saw he was driving resolutely towards the shallow patch. Is it surprising that we allowed ourselves a chortle or two when the boat came to a halt so abruptly that his next order was cut off short as he winded himself on the wheel? Can you really cry shame because, when he looked around for a tow, we were all back in our fusty sleeping bags, hugging our hangovers?

Just why should this veiled animosity exist? My theory is that it's all a matter of that old monster — one-upmanship. Each skipper, and come to that each crew member, wants to be recognised as the real driving force behind the team. But he knows (life being the way it is) that the chances of winning and retaining such status are granted to only a few — we're not all Moitessiers, after all. So watching somebody else bounce off the harbour wall gives him a warm glow of superiority, if he managed to miss it on this occasion, or a reassurance that he's not the sole idiot in the place if he didn't, and was himself spotted backing off, red-faced, earlier in the day.

The racing skipper will be careful to make all the right noises about the loyalty and devotion of his crew — "Couldn't have done it without 'em. Fine bunch of keen lads", and so on — but at the same time he'll like it to be well broadcast just who is the decision maker and, closer to his heart perhaps, just who signs the cheques. The crew, mindful of the need to retain their berths aboard, will be quick to pile praise on the skipper's head — "Stalwart leadership. A calm, commanding presence in times of trial", and all that — but they want it known, and take subtle steps to ensure that it is, just how well the Old Boy would have fared if he'd been left to himself.

We cruising types are no better. We regale our shore-based friends with stirring (and improbable) tales of the perils of the deep and our skill in dealing with them. We bask in their cries of envy and admiration and we hope, loudly and hypocritically, that they'll be free to join us for a sail one of these days. In truth, there's little we desire less. For one thing, the reason we became addicted to the nautical life in the first place was that it removed us from the company of everyday mortals like them and into a world where we could live out our sea-faring fantasies. Allow them to witness the reality and where's your reputation gone then?

Sooner or later, though, you'll have to live up to your promises — and to all those fine stories — by taking a visitor along. Suddenly, you're in a whole new world. We see a side of our friends, and by golly they see a side of us, that neither would have believed possible in normal circumstances. It can show itself in many ways. They may know us as hard-headed, go-getting business types and be stunned to find us suddenly turned into soft-eyed romantics, quoting poetry, waxing lyrical over a rainbow through the mist, and sipping Campbell's Cream of Tomato as if it were the food of the gods. Likewise, we may assume them to be ignorant, pen-pushing landlubbers only to discover that beneath that pin-stripe suit beats the heart of a budding Knox-Johnston, just longing for an opportunity to show all the inborn skills that made Britain one of the great sea-faring nations of history.

Such rapid readjustments must be expected to lead to tensions. I've yet to meet the skipper who wholeheartedly welcomes a stranger on board, although some are better at disguising their misgivings than others. The snag for the newcomer is that he wants to feel a part of the gang, even though he knows that the gang is well used to functioning without him. If he just hangs around he's only going to feel he's in the way — and he will be. All the gang wants, on the other hand, is to have him as a spellbound audience while they show off.

Someone has to take responsibility for the visitor — and it's unlikely to be the skipper. The weight of command usually hangs especially heavy on his shoulders when there's a guest to entertain and he'll off-load this task, even if it was at his personal invitation that the chap's there at all, onto a lesser crew member, the woman being the obvious choice. This has the double advantage of both establishing the skipper as the great untouchable, and giving him someone else to blame if the novice falls overboard, acquires a hernia, or fractures his skull on a passing boom. "I assigned *you* to look after him. Do I have to do *everything* myself?"

One technique which I've found handy is to broach the ship's liquor stores immediately on leaving port and keep the visitor half-sozzled for the duration of his stay, provided of course that he's securely lashed into place. This gives him a feeling of benign well-being and contentment, recognisable by a silly smirk which just occasionally gives way to a look of intense concentration as he tries to work out whether it's the state of the sea, or of the gin bottle, that's making the table heave about so alarmingly. If he should take it into his head to get up and wander about, the effort required simply to stay upright will discourage any attempts to take a hand in things, so blunders are minimised. Better yet, if when he finally staggers ashore he has any unflattering reports to make about the conduct of the ship's company, his obvious state of intoxication will render them less credible to one's sailing cronies.

A kinder, and certainly a cheaper, way to control this potential disaster area is to give the new man something to do — at least then you know where he is, and he has the impression that he's making a contribution. It's a false impression, but no matter about that, and again if things go wrong you can blame him. But what job on board ship is really suitable for the untried man? All regular crews, regardless of their levels of competence, have evolved their own little ways of doing things which a newcomer can only learn by time and the weary process of trial and error. For the hapless visitor it's highly likely to be the error side that gets the upper hand.

Put him out of the way on the foredeck and you've got a real pantomime on your hands. The skipper is in the cockpit bawling urgent and, to the new boy, entirely incomprehensible instructions. The regular foredeck hand is twitching with frustration and dividing his time between rolling his eyes to heaven and making brief little forays halfway along the side deck and back again. "Leave him alone, Joe. He's got to learn," advises the skipper, as if this exile to the pointy end were the

Laughing fellow rovers.

modern-day equivalent of a couple of hours in the stocks. And all the while the novice, seeking further enlightenment or perhaps some crumb of comfort, keeps appearing and reappearing on either side of the mast like the wicked Baron trailing the Babes in the Wood.

Put him on a winch and he'll soon render it invisible under a pile-up of riding turns, probably including the strings of his anorak and a fair amount of ripped fingernail, and then secure the dead end by tying a granny knot around the drum. He may be pleased to be invited to take the tiller but the first few minutes in the hot seat will rapidly wipe the smile off his face. Suddenly he's the centre of attention, everyone aboard will feel they could do it better and any number of unidentified hands will close over his to urge him gently this way or that. He, however, will be aware only of the hoarse breathing coming from just behind him, as the skipper fights back the urge to scream.

Send him below to give instrument readings, and you have to double check everything he says. Otherwise you may find, as we once did, that a steady call of "five fathoms, five fathoms . . ." is followed by a grinding bounce off something solid which hurls you straight down the companionway and face-to-aggrieved-face with him. "But it *did* say five until a second ago", he complains bitterly, pointing to the electric log which, you're forced grudgingly to admit, does bear a passing resemblance to the echosounder if one is not used to such things.

When all else fails, the skipper can either give up and leave the poor chap to stew in isolation, feeling about as useful on board as a sack of fertiliser, or else he can quickly pass the buck to his lady and send the novice to give her a hand in the galley. She cringes inwardly as she hears his enthusiastic agreement to this plan: "Oh great idea! I'm quite a dab hand in the kitchen, though I say so myself." She can look forward to her corned beef hash being salted three times, her bread rolls being scattered far and wide, and that most terrifying of sights — the

68

newcomer balancing precariously on the companionway steps clutching a saucepan filled to the brim with boiling gravy. "Where do you want me to put this?" he asks innocently, and may well get an answer he doesn't expect to hear from a lady.

Oddest of all is that at the end of the day, when the party is breaking up, this maligned and humiliated being will turn round as he's cautiously lowering himself into the dinghy and offer his undying thanks. Not, you can bet, to the long-suffering lady who has guided and guarded him, fed and watered him, and given him sympathetic consolation when he's been careless, stupid, frightened or sick. ("Don't feel too bad. Honestly, it happens to us all at some time!") No, it's the skipper who'll get all the gratitude for this wonderful, enriching experience.

And he'll lap it up too. Incandescent with joy at getting shot of the visitor at last, he'll clap him on the back and cry with every evidence of sincerity, "Not at all, old chap. Great pleasure to have you, and you really got the hang of things. Don't know how we'd have managed without you!"

Only the crew hears his parting remark, however, as the dinghy pulls away. "But next time, we'll try!"

8

Travellers' tales

As someone — possibly me — once said, sailing stories should always be taken with a pinch of the Old Salt. It's not that we're barefaced liars by nature; it's just that the tales we pick for re-telling tend to be the ones that show us and our skills as seamen and women in the best light — and if they don't they are suitably doctored. Having listened to both my skipper and me recounting the highlights of our summer cruise, friends have sometimes raised doubts as to whether we were actually travelling on the same boat.

To overcome this, we've developed a system whereby he sticks to the 'us against the elements' stories and I have a free hand in the shore-based ones. This is fair enough, as he, like many cruising skippers I've met, regards every hour spent in leisurely exploration of the places he's come through such hell to visit as an hour wasted. Having arrived somewhere, his thoughts immediately turn to the next harbour on the list, and the challenges to be met along the way.

To my skipper, the only stops worth making are those to take on vital supplies — food, fuel and fresh water — and the need to do the laundry, grab a bath and a hairwash or admire the scenery are all dismissed as idle feminine indulgences. He reckons the scenery always looks better from a couple of miles offshore anyway. And even when we do agree on a halt he'll pass the buck of the necessary provisioning onto other

shoulders — mine — preferring to 'stay with the boat, in case of emergencies'. If pushed, he may consent to carry a load of groceries or a bag of damp washing on the often lengthy hike to and from the nearest settlement but he'll do it with all the cheerful willingness of an aged bulldog transporting a soggy mouthful of morning paper.

To get at the truth of what cruising is really like, it's best to begin at the beginning — and that's long before the boat actually sets sail. In the weeks beforehand, my skipper tends to be absent from home quite a bit 'to make ready the boat'. At least, that's what he says he's been doing when he wanders in with a slightly vacuous smile just after closing time. Meanwhile I'm fighting a losing battle to have everything wanted-on-voyage clean, counted and ready for the big day. We draw up long, complicated lists which are later scrapped, since we duplicate the obvious items and find ourselves locked in bitter argument about the more personal needs expressed in each other's inventory. *He* can't see why I should insist on six changes of clothes per person, plus toys, games, books, spare teddy bears and enough stores for a small expeditionary force. *I* take a dim view of being asked to appear publicly with one who thinks all foreseeable requirements of dress are covered by an extra sweater, half a motheaten track suit and a change of underpants, all shoved in a polythene bag.

71

I also have to take a firm stand on the inclusion of shaving gear; my skipper has a persistent yearning to grow a resplendent beard while at sea. In fact, the end result isn't too bad — he was once mistaken for Robin Knox-Johnston and has never forgotten it — but the preliminary stages take some bearing. With a seven-day growth, he lacks only blackened teeth and a meths bottle protruding from the smock pocket to qualify for a place in a queue for the soup-kitchen. Bank cashiers turn over his credit card with undisguised scepticism.

The loading of stores is the next hurdle. As the locker space diminishes and the pile of bags and boxes on the jetty seems unchanged, the potential for trouble increases. It reaches a crisis around the point I discover a private store of Guinness in the bread bin, or he finds three spare packs of cornflakes in the chart locker. As a *coup de grâce*, a cardboard box rendered soggy by the trip in the dinghy will jettison its contents into the sea and it's either back to the shops or do without bacon, butter and tea for a week.

Weather permitting, our departure usually takes place on schedule but in a state of semi-chaos and with attitudes of extreme martyrdom on all sides. But once away, a new mood of optimism sets in, misplaced though it no doubt is. With telephones, bank statements and other minor irritants of everyday life behind us, we find we can easily turn our attention to getting things shipshape and looking forward to the idyllic time that lies ahead. Take our six-week cruise to the Outer Hebrides, for instance. As the Irish coastline faded astern, we had such a clear picture of what lay ahead. We'd proceed to Stornoway at a cracking and invigorating pace, and there we'd stock up, take a breather, and then meander gently southwards again, overnighting where the mood took us, drinking in the views, fishing a little, sunbathing a lot, relaxing a little more each day until we arrived home bronzed, fit, restored and tranquil.

Like a lot of cruising schedules, this one relied heavily on the assumption of good weather. It didn't seem much to ask — just

"I've been getting the boat ready . . ."

blue skies, calm seas, wind no stronger than a moderate breeze and always from the right direction. In the event, what we got was a daily choice between beating hard into rain, spray and strengthening winds or waiting for a clearance and then wallowing along under engine through a sickening residual swell, without a breath of wind to steady us, after the blow had passed. In between came long spells riding to anchor, or two anchors, or two anchors plus a heavy weight along the chain.

Under these circumstances, crew relationships were severely tested and, it must be admitted, often found wanting. As the outward journey became extended into a series of brief port-to-port hops, with an accumulated mileage sadly below our intentions, the skipper and I became increasingly tetchy. Fortunately the children were more adaptable — which was odd. At home, with warmth, comfort, TV and a vast stock of toys to amuse them they exist in a constant state of mutual hostility. But stormbound in some isolated Hebridean wilderness with only the resources of a small, damp boat and two weary parents at their disposal, they would play in ear-shattering harmony for hours on end. Even the dog, an inbred neurotic since puppyhood, would shuffle himself into a sleeping bag, sigh deeply, and settle down to the task of remaining inconspicuous until actually booted out for a relief-giving walk amid the wet heather.

For the skipper and me, relief did not come so easily. Even when conditions were such that no sensible boat, short-handed as ours is, would dream of putting to sea, we still couldn't resign ourselves to our fate. We'd watch the skies interminably for the tiniest break in the cloud cover, and greet each minute speck of blue as if it heralded the start of a heat wave. We'd poke our heads out of the hatch into a blast that plastered the hair down flat and inhibited normal breathing and then retire below to assure each other that "it seems to be easing off a bit". Weather forecasts were tape-recorded and played and replayed while we listened with intense concentration, trying to extract new meaning from the familiar words, like a pair of cloistered academics giving some obscure Anglo-Saxon text a thorough going-over.

The only way to relieve the tension was to find some useful activity to pursue, and it will come as no surprise to learn that the jobs the skipper and I elected to do always proved mutually incompatible. I find that when under stress of this kind, the general precariousness of our situation gives a firm prod to my normally dormant female nesting instincts and I like to scrub and tidy and throw out rubbish with great ruthlessness. The skipper, on the other hand, likes to take dirty objects apart and spread them about the place.

No matter how sweetly the engine may have been turning

74

over for the last hundred or so nautical miles, on a bad day there is always some slight symptom of potential trouble which requires immediate investigation. Bits of machinery are systematically lined up on bunks, floor and table top where they each spread an individual pool of black oil and await the inevitable scattering by my elbows, the dog's feet, or small inquisitive fingers. We can usually guarantee that at the end of the cruise some unidentifiable piece of metal will be retrieved from the bilges with no clue as to whether it originated in the engine, the echosounder or the flushing mechanism for the loo.

A typical clash of interests occurred when we'd at last managed to claw our way as far as South Rona and were waiting for a suitable day to cross the Minch to the Outer Isles. It was a three-day wait and South Rona, while well sheltered, had little to offer in entertainment terms — it's uninhabited for a start, and at the time of our stay had the added attributes of being cold, wet, enshrouded by mist, and host to a plague of midges so dense that you couldn't set foot ashore without breathing in a thousand or two. Vital stores were running low so it seemed an ideal time to give in to those motherly instincts of mine and bake some fresh, crusty bread. Comfort food, the psychologists would call it.

No sooner had I got the mix under way and the table top floured ready for the kneading process than the skipper threw himself down beside me, our precious autopilot clasped in his itchy fingers. True, it had been a trifle erratic in its guidance but we'd learned to compensate for its occasional whims, and getting home without this undemanding extra hand could be a trying experience.

"I thought I'd just have a little look. I won't touch anything that looks complex", the skipper reassured me, easing the tip of a screwdriver into the casing.

"Are you quite sure you know what you're . . ." I began, but before I could complete the question there was a sharp crack and my dough was sprayed with such a confusion of springs,

75

ratchets and ballbearings that we could hardly believe they'd all come from such a tiny gap in the cover.

The skipper's reaction was remarkably mild, considering the size of the mess. But then, he was to pay for his foolhardiness. Not only did he have to bear the brunt of the hand-steering that was our lot for the rest of the trip, but he also found on our return that the manufacturers were less than keen to honour their guarantee on an instrument which, despite his protestations of innocence, plainly had half its innards missing. For me, however, the sad demise of our automatic helmsman proved a blessing in disguise since it decreased the length of sailing periods and increased the number of landfalls to rest and recharge our spirits.

But landfalls bring their own traumas on our boat, again largely because of our divergent attitudes. I'll dash to the pilot book and start reading and rereading the instructions while we're still all of five miles off, working up a healthy neurosis and planning out a course around rocks and headlands which are as yet invisible in the murk ahead. The skipper, with some justification, reckons that I do enough panicking for two and goes to the other extreme, trusting to luck and the theory that the shortest distance between two points is always a straight line. Left to himself, he'll spot a mast — which may later transpire to be a telegraph pole — and make a beeline for it regardless of intervening obstacles, until a terrified squeal from a child posted on the foredeck prompts a rapid change of direction. The alternative, under my frenzied directions, is for the boat to make her approach through a series of apparently motiveless twists and turns, like a demented bumblebee looking for a likely blossom to alight on. Already anchored crews, watching our tortuous wanderings, assume we're either drunk or in difficulties.

"Got a problem with the steering, have you?" they enquire solicitously as we stumble past them.

"You can say that again," says the skipper, with some venom. "Have you met my wife . . .?"

Bank cashiers turn over his card with undisguised scepticism.

I will admit that I do have a phobia about pilot books. Although the skipper constantly assures me that they are written with extreme eventualities in mind — say a fifty-footer with no engine and a twelve-foot draft approaching against wind and tide in thick fog — I still can't treat their dire warnings of hidden horrors with the same cheering scepticism he employs. And it's not hard to see why: on the day we do clobber something, I know exactly who'll get the blame.

Take the time we were heading into Ardminish Bay, on Gigha Island. This is one of our favourite haunts so, although the pilot book specifically advises one not to make the turn until well abeam the old ferry pier, the skipper decided we could play it cool and cut the corner — possibly because it was getting on for opening time. Some of this cockiness must have rubbed off on me, for I blithely counted off the exposed rocks and said, "OK, in we go!" just as the ferry swept past. Her crew waved violently. "Yoo hoo!" we chorused, pleased by the welcome. They waved more violently and it was then I noticed that the seagull directly in our path was not, as I had first thought, bobbing about on the waves but strolling casually around on something very solid. We did actually miss the reef by a barnacle, but for weeks afterwards I had to cope with the skipper's little jibes. To the children, "The next time we go ashore we must get a few new toys for you — and a counting frame for Mummy." To visiting crews, "Oh, we each have our own responsibilities on this boat — my wife does the navigating and I do the skid turns." And to our own club cronies, "Well, no need to scrub off the anti-fouling this season. Les scraped it off bit by bit while we were away."

Equally maddening is the fact that when you return from your bold ocean venture, and start to swap sailing tales with your fellow rovers, no matter how well you've fared in your travels they've always had a better time than you. Or so they say.

"Oh, didn't you like So-and-So Town?" they query in simulated astonishment. "We had the most marvellous night

78

there — and met some *super* people!" (We, on the other hand, spent a dreary hour tramping through a downpour trying to buy a pint of milk and a can of diesel, and met only a wet dog and a hostile harbourmaster who told us we couldn't tie up *there*, and fees would be four pounds fifty, thank you very much.)

"Of course, *we* were there for the Regatta/Golf Tournament/ Beer Festival/state visit of the Royal Yacht Britannia . . ." they add, smugly, as if this were the result of superb advance planning rather than happy coincidence. The only events that coincide with *our* arrivals in port are usually a water shortage, a bin-men's strike, or early closing day. All we need is a pub sign which says 'No singing. No dancing. No children allowed.' and our happiness is complete.

"Oh, come on now," say our friends, nudging us knowingly, "There's you and the skipper . . . I mean, a man and a woman . . . surely you can think up some entertaining way of passing the time . . . hmmm?" Well, we can certainly *think* about it. Putting it into practice is, however, another matter entirely.

9

And then there are more delicate matters . . .

It's frequently stated that there is no closer relationship than that between shipmates. Taken literally, this can't be disputed. Within the confines of a small boat you really don't have much alternative to rubbing shoulders — and other more intimate parts of the anatomy — with your fellow crew. One person working at the galley, another plotting fixes at the chart table, and a third lurching down the companionway steps grabbing for anything that will offer support can lead to violent impromptu wrestling bouts with squeals, apologies and red faces all round.

You get used to it in time, although the more bashful members of the company may resort to ludicrous contortions in order to avoid blush-making displays of naked flesh. Our son, approaching his teens and suddenly conscious of his dignity, dresses each morning by snaking out an arm, snatching his pile of clothing and retreating with it into his sleeping bag where he worms his way into his garments, like some cave-dwelling predator grappling with its prey. Most of us, however, learn to adjust our levels of modesty and cease to care if, despite elephantine waving of sleeves and much grunting and wriggling, taking off our smock top brings the sweater along too revealing us to a battery of fascinated eyes in all our topless glory. Privacy it seems, is yet another commodity you have to do without when you go sailing.

But there are times when it's just what you need, even amongst the most laid-back and broadminded crews. Cooping up males and females together, often scantily clad, invigorated by fresh air and the call of the wild, or simply, as we've seen, in need of a means of passing the waiting hours; all these lead to just one thing — of which more in a moment. First there's a more down-to-earth, more frequent, and indeed more pressing need to consider — and that's a visit to the heads.

Men don't suffer in the same way as women. Without going into sordid biological detail, it's clear that the nifty layout of the male anatomy means that when Nature calls all that's needed is a casual stroll to the foredeck, perhaps with a throw-away request that the more sensitive crew members should briefly transfer their gaze elsewhere. It's not so simple for the ladies who, clad in oilies, jeans and a couple of layers of woolly undies, require both time and seclusion if we're to accomplish our aim (and I choose that word deliberately) with any semblance of dignity and efficiency.

On my very first keelboat outing, for example, we had a fine breeze, a crew of four hearty males, a generous supply of home-brew, and no loo. As the bottles emptied and the level of merriment grew, one by one the men slipped off to 'examine the cut of the jib' and return, much relieved. I meanwhile went from gaiety through vague discomfort and on to acute distress before one of my pals recognised the symptoms of impending kidney failure, handed me a galvanised bucket and pointed towards the saloon. It was then that I discovered the basic design faults in both sailing clothes and female construction. With thick layers of lowered garments forming a tight, unyielding band at knee level it was impossible to balance myself against the lively rolling of the boat and at the same time to form any kind of working relationship with the bucket. A series of swift tacking manoeuvres, no doubt vastly amusing to those on deck, soon had me and the bucket crashing about together on the floor and left me with Freudian inhibitions for life.

It was a relief, in every sense, to find our next boat had some of the comforts of home, even though to get to the heads you had to double over and shuffle forward like a reluctant pot-holer. It had a huge flushing handle with a big black knob, apparently poised to strike anyone who did not observe, to the letter, the precisely worded instructions printed in bold type and heavily underlined in red. Indeed we sometimes wondered what would happen to any independent spirit who refused to 'pump repeatedly and vigorously with lid closed' — would he perhaps be engulfed in a sea of dilute sewage in the small hours? Our own robust pumping eventually caused the black knob to fly off and disappear into the bilges, where it resisted all attempts at rescue and amused itself instead by cantering about infuriatingly during the quiet reaches of a night at anchor.

The instructions, however, said nothing about adjusting dress before leaving, and just as well since the most agile contortionist would have had trouble there. Standing was not on, so one's lower clothing had to be retrieved in stages, ankles to knees while still seated, then knees to waist while kneeling as if in prayer. Visitors not practised in such skills would be found rolling about the floor, heaving on a zip and gasping like snake-bite victims in the final death throes. The forehatch was too far away to ease the problem, but close enough to mean that unless one gave the entire crew due notice of one's activities there was the real possibility of receiving an unwelcome visitor from on high or of being smothered in billows of wet genoa during a sail change.

On our next craft, the hatch was directly overhead, which helped a little, as you could get more leeway by shoving your top half out into the elements. This provided some useful ventilation, and also meant you need never feel alone as your apparently disembodied head could engage in matey banter with the deckhands. On the debit side, though, you often got a belt round the ear from a wildly flapping jib, and if the boat should dip her nose into a big green one, you could cop a couple of gallons clean down your spine, generally at quite the wrong psychological moment. Further, it was possible (and I proved it) when dropping through the forehatch to jam both feet in the toilet bowl, winding up with two sprained ankles and a pair of highly insanitary deckshoes. I was trying to bid a cheery farewell to a tearstained party of concerned relatives on the harbour wall when it happened. Instead of heading out to sea with a nonchalant wave, I disappeared through the trap with a startled scream, like the Demon King in a village panto.

There was space aplenty in our next loo. This converted fishing smack had heads in which you could not only stand up, but also swing a larger-than-average cat, should the mood take you. The toilet was mounted on a pedestal like a museum exhibit with a grained mahogany seat and gleaming brass fittings. Flushing it required Herculean strength, and the decaying gaskets produced a Niagara of minor leaks. Behind it was the locker housing our massive anchor chain, which gave out sepulchral groans and clanks with each movement of the boat. On a dark night, with a chill atmosphere and glistening condensation all around, one expected a flight of bats and a ghostly apparition at any second.

Modern design has tried to overcome the privacy problem, with mixed results. Our present loo is shut off from the saloon, so its use does not unduly upset the flavour of the evening meal. But it's open to the forepeak so anyone unwise enough to try to catch a few hours' kip in the berth there is likely to suffer an unsavoury visitation or else be booted unceremoniously from his bunk.

An alternative is to have a series of narrow doors which open into and against each other according to which compartment you wish to isolate. These result in bewilderment for the visitor, occasional squashed fingers even for the initiated, and incipient claustrophobia for all. But having succeeded in giving us a tiny bit of privacy, the designers can't leave well alone and cram the available space with little 'extras' to give the feminine touch. "The lady in your life will love the luxury, glide-away vanitory unit and sink," trill the advertisements. Not when it comes careering out when least expected and gives her a hearty clout across the back of the head, she won't. Or what about those mirror-fronted lockers they insist on mounting over the loo? The mirror is never in the right spot to be functional — unless you happen to be obsessed with viewing your navel — and the contents of the locker have a sneaky way of shifting around on passage so that sliding back the door produces a shower of toothbrushes, hairgrips and one's private supply of Valium into the toilet below. If they're not rescued immediately, the flush will cease to work and someone will have to face the vile task of dismantling the system and groping around in its evil depths to clear the blockage. The lucky candidate will be rewarded by having to eat dinner alone for a week.

Perhaps the biggest hang-ups come when you're a visitor at a convivial gathering on a strange boat. You slope off to the heads, trying to escape notice. You do what you have to, fervently hoping the gay revelry next door will drown out the unavoidable sound effects — like rain on a tin roof (funny how they always run out of conversation just at the vital moment). Then you try to flush it; and you never can get it right can you? Of course, there's now total silence next door as they all exchange knowing smiles. Eventually, after increasingly desperate efforts have failed to produce a result, you have to

"Will you want these hairgrips again?"

emerge, blushing and sheepish, and ask a total stranger to make up for your inadequacies.

But if this enforced intimacy is a problem, how much worse are the occasions when a little bit of intimacy is just what takes your fancy — or would, given half a chance. From watching the TV sailing programmes or Boat Show reports, the novice might think that we're into one of the sexiest sports around. Nubile blondes in scanty bikinis stretching out on the foredeck while husky, weathered skippers flex their muscles at the helm — the togetherness, the thrills of salt spray on the face and cool wind in the hair, must surely arouse some primitive urges, both male and female? The boats themselves have undeniable sex-appeal, as the sharp prow slices incisively through the waves which lick their way deliciously along the sleek curves of the hull to join in a creamy, turbulent wake at the stern. The mast stands tall and proud, thrusting powerfully upward. The symbolism is inescapable, isn't it?

Ah yes, but those of us who actually go sailing know only too well that all is not as it would seem to the envious outsider. Should you believe that after a day of setting heavy sails, hauling on wet ropes, straining every muscle to stay upright in a lively sea we then spend our nights thrashing around enjoying a bit of sexual mayhem, let me put you right. For a start, those skimpy bikinis may be grand for shore-based enticement, but get to sea anywhere around our own coastal waters and you'll soon be frantically searching in your locker for vest, long johns, fleecy pants and a thick sweater, all topped off with oil-skins — garments guaranteed to make your figure look like a Russian shot-putter.

Even if the mood did suddenly grab you, by the time you'd stripped that lot off it would have passed for sure. He could help, of course, which could be an arousing experience, but not when he has to ram a booted foot into your stomach to get extra purchase on your jacket sleeves. And have you ever tried to run your fingers alluringly through the tumbled curls of your dream man after a day at sea? It's like trying to untangle a knotted fishing line. Exchange a fond kiss and the flavour is reminiscent of salted herrings, well past their best. And how about those hands, with which you hope he'll caress your softly yielding body? Unless he's the sort of chap who goes in for lashings of Nivea and white cotton gloves at night (and there aren't too many of *them* on the sailing scene, let me tell you) then your quick roll in the sack will leave you feeling more as if you'd had a smart rub-down with a bit of coarse-grain wet-and-dry.

But what the hell! We're tough girls, we sailing types. We

Skimpy bikinis may be fine for shore-based enticement . . .

can take it when the going gets rough, and there's no doubt that the enlivening sea air, the healthy uninhibited life of the sailor, the boredom of a long passage, *can* all combine to give the old libido a bit of a nudge in the right direction. But the questions are, when and where?

As to when; well, if you're racing you can forget it! Most skippers easily sublimate their baser desires to the thrills of competitive sailing, and the rest of the crew may feel that the chance of a bit of voyeurism en route is not adequate compensation for limping across the finishing line with the dregs of the fleet. For the cruising types the chances are better, but you'll still need a crew that is either very discreet or very broadminded, or failing that, extremely reliable self-steering. In shipping lanes, or fishing grounds, it would be a most foolhardy, or highly frustrated, couple who would take the risk.

It certainly helps to be the exhibitionist type — and I'm not. We were cruising once off a deserted stretch of West Cork coastline when I felt a sudden need for a cooling shower. I lined up soap, towel and a supply of icy fresh water, happily stripped off in the cockpit under the fascinated gaze of husband and kids, and raised the first bucket above my head. I thought I could hear cheers as the water cascaded down but it was only as I shook the drops from my eyes that I realised that my audience comprised not only my own family but the deckhands of a local trawler, leering from the siderail as they went charging past. They did a skid turn and came back for a second look, which I suppose was flattering, but by then I was cowering damply in the saloon and stayed there until they were once more a dot on the horizon.

If sex at sea is a non-starter, that leaves the *après*-sail period, when you're safe at anchor or tied up at the quayside. Let's set aside for the sake of argument the fact that once you've spent an hour making sure the boat is properly snugged down for the night (vital for safety), and cooked and eaten a large meal (vital for harmony and health), and drunk several large Scotches (vital for my peace of mind) all you feel like is crawling into your bunk and snoring till dawn. Assuming instead that the spirit is willing, you are still stuck with the old problem of privacy, or rather the lack of it.

On a still, balmy night when neither wind nor tide stirs the calm waters of the anchorage, it can be painfully obvious to the neighbouring crews that the rhythmic motions of one lonely craft indicate that there's more than sleep going on below decks. If you're tied up alongside another boat it's worse. The hulls of modern craft are not thick, and if you can hear the next-door skipper cracking his morning egg into the pan, just imagine what a fascinating sound picture your own activities must have been giving him the night before. It makes conversation a trifle stilted, to say the least.

But even if your timing is OK, you still have the question of where to carry out your plans. Few and far between are the boats which offer spacious double-bed accommodation. Bunks are more often tucked away behind, on top of or beneath something or other and provide minimum room for one person, in a tight-fitting sleeping bag, to grab a few hours' kip — nothing else. It can be quite traumatic if, at the critical moment, your loved one suddenly rockets into the air with a howl of agony because his unprotected rear end has come into vicious and nerve-shattering contact with the sharp edge of the chart table.

Not many boats carry such refinements as satin sheets, fur rugs and feather quilts either. We nautical types go in for sleeping bags, which are pretty limiting just for sleeping in, never mind any more frolicsome activities. Get two of you thrashing about inside, even if it's a fancy job that zips alongside another to make a double, and you're soon hopelessly lost in a tangle of arms, legs and quilted nylon. And it doesn't help if the boat is not the only lady around who tends to be a bit broad in the beam. As a friend of mine put it: "Sex on board is not for the broad. It is far less harrowing for the fairly narrowing." How true, how true.

When I researched the same subject with my male acquaintances, I found them strangely reticent, reacting only with nudges, knowing leers and winks which fooled nobody. Only one had the guts to tell the truth — a lusty lad who leaves you in no doubt when ashore that his heart, and indeed his more salient features, are in the right place.

"Writing about sex and sailing?" he queried scornfully. "Just put down the title, leave the pages blank, and you'll have the whole scene in a nutshell. In fact, I really don't know why we bring you women along at all!"

I rest my case.

10

Females afloat

It was a typical scene at the end of a sailing day. The boat was in a state of mild chaos, the kids were squabbling, and the skipper and I were hardly more affable, having arrived at the canal entrance to find the gates closed with no clue whether the keeper had gone for a quick pint, or home for the weekend.

We'd just tied up to a handy jetty when another yacht hove into view. A trim craft she was, all new, neat and shiny with sails and warps with the pristine cleanliness of recent purchase. Similarly the crew (plainly a husband and wife team) were dressed in glowing, stain-free oilies, matching tie-up boots, and jaunty whiter-than-white woolly caps. There was a moment's wobbly hesitation as they too discovered the closed lock gates, and then the decision: "We'll go alongside that other boat, my love."

"Oooh!" she squeaked. "What shall I do, darling?"

Under his gentle direction she scampered up and down the decks, laying out warps at bow and stern, and with a barely audible crunch — excusable as the wind was rising — we acquired some new neighbours.

"Now what shall I do, sweetheart?" she queried, hanging on to our guardrails with an anxious expression.

"Hand over the bow warp, darling." She complied with a winning smile. "Now the stern warp, pet. No, it goes through the fairlead, remember?"

The job done, she straightened up and surveyed her handiwork with satisfaction. "There! All safe and sound. Now, a nice cup of coffee, don't you think?" And she nipped below to attend to her domestic duties, humming a happy little tune. But, just as we heard the first tenuous wail of the kettle coming to the boil, the lock gates swung open.

"Right, we're off!" said my skipper, impatient for his long overdue dinner. "You first," he encouraged the newcomers.

"Ah, good, yes . . . er . . . could you come up, darling? We're going in now." Instantly 'darling' appeared, the kettle's whistle coming to an abrupt halt. More scampering as she dashed to let go at bow and stern, and then delighted at having got it right she disappeared below, presumably back to her coffee-brewing.

As she did so, it all happened at once. The wind, now piping up strongly, caught them broadside and the boat heeled sharply, with the muffled tinkling of breaking crockery. The rush of water from the lock hit the bows slewing them round head-on to the sea wall, and the top three feet of their hastily stowed jib, which had been shuttling up and down the forestay, suddenly filled, giving them quite an impressive turn of speed towards the rocks.

"Aaah, you bitch!" hissed the skipper, turning the same shade as his hat. A flushed face appeared from the hatchway.

"Can I do something, darling?"

"Yes, you damned well can!" we heard him bellow. "You can start the bloody engine. You're standing next to the sodding thing!"

˙Luckily, the engine responded at once and they reached the lock in safety, but the domestic storm did not subside for we could still hear his agonised cries: "Fenders, woman, for God's sake where are the fenders? Haven't you got that blasted heaving line ready? What the hell do you mean, what does it look like?"

By the time we joined them, the situation was under control, and so was the lady, but only just. Eyes brimming, she was standing grasping the forestay as if her life depended on it.

91

"Oh dear", she ventured, offering me a brave, if watery, smile. "I'm afraid he does get rather cross at times. This is all new to me, you see."

I wanted to offer her some crumb of comfort, to assure her that the histrionic performance we'd just witnessed was not in the least unusual, that had she been sailing twenty years she could have confidently expected the same treatment, that merely stepping aboard a boat could turn the most harmonious male-female relationship into a searing battleground. And I *would* have told her, too, except that as I drew in breath to begin the sluices opened with a violent upheaval of water, and I, having dropped the shoreline in order to gesticulate and emphasise my points, suddenly found I was in my own all-action situation while my skipper poured scorn and wrath upon my head. After that, nothing needed to be said; we swapped grimaces of bitter understanding — sisters under the oilskins.

But it only goes oilskin deep, this instant fellow-feeling between sailing women. Despite the apparent similarities, underneath it all we have just as much individuality and eccentricity as do our menfolk. An anthropologist in search of exotic human behaviour might well abandon his studies of tribal rituals in darkest Africa in favour of an in-depth appraisal of the membership of your average yacht club.

Look around any club bar, when the crews gather to relax from their seagoing exertions, and you can plainly spot the differences emerging. There are the cruising types, for instance, clustered together to 'benefit from each other's experiences' or, to put it more accurately, swapping highly embroidered and somewhat dubious accounts of their own courage in the face of adversity or waxing lyrical about the perfection of remote anchorages as yet unknown to the writers of pilot books. My skipper is a prime example.

"Had the place all to ourselves. Wonderful feeling of isolation . . . closeness to nature . . . that's what it's all about . . ." he'll enthuse, brandishing a snapshot of a tiny speck that may or may not be our yacht, anchored in lashing rain in a cheerless,

Giving them an impressive turn of speed . . .

rockstrewn pool that we entered by accident and got out of only by great good fortune.

Meanwhile your racing types are in another group, adopting aggressive postures, slopping the froth off their pints as they lean forward to poke each other in the chest and dispute for the umpteenth time the rights and wrongs of a protest that was turned down all of three weeks ago. And huddled at a table set a little apart from the common herd, shrouded in mystery and tobacco smoke, we find the club politicians. Their discussions are conducted in sly undertones, lest the rest of us should become aware either of the triviality of the topic or of the real nature of what we have fondly imagined to be club democrácy.

Women tend to be the minority in these cliques — although the more vociferous of us may have leading roles. Exclusively female, however, is the group of selfless toilers, the worker bees in the complex structure of yacht club society. They will

93

generally be found with their heads together mulling over their next task, be it the construction of a new rota for taking home and washing the roller towels, or evaluating the precise number of sausages required for the Children's Day beanfeast. I've been party to discussions, stretching until closing time, in which the central topic was nothing more momentous than how many adults, teens and tots could reasonably be fed from one bag of frozen chips. These ladies are justifiably popular around the club, as their contribution to the social scene is beyond question. Their sea-going qualities, though, may be less apparent.

Take our Edna, for instance. Her family boat is without doubt the most spick and span in the anchorage — not only are the carpets ever-spotless but I've heard it rumoured that the bilges get a weekly Hoovering too — and around the club, she's the one who scrubs out the showers, sponges the Guinness from the walls, boils up the tea-urn for post-racing refreshments, and much more. But when the cruising season begins in earnest she is happy, indeed anxious, to take a back seat. Just as the crew are completing their final preparations prior to departure, she'll come staggering along the pierhead clutching in one hand a plastic box of home-made rock cakes, guaranteed to explode into a cascade of crumbs onto the cockpit sole at the first bite, and in the other a still-hissing pressure cooker. This latter contains a glutinous stew so full of onions in an attempt to eke out a meagre meat ration that the unfortunate crew are destined to spend their first night at sea gulping back great blasts of flatulence or beating a tattoo on the door of the occupied heads, with strangled cries of internal agony. Then, her duty done, she'll wave them a fond, and very firm, farewell.

Despite Edna's example, it would be quite wrong to assume that women only go sailing when they have been either bribed or press-ganged into it. Many actually do take to the sport in a big way — or at least strive very hard to give that impression, often going way over the top in their efforts to prove that there is no real difference between the sexes and that daring,

94

"Luckily I was able to put him right. Chay, I said . . ."

toughness and grit are not all on the male side. You'll recognise us — my friends assure me that I must include myself in this category — by our no-nonsense, workmanlike clothing, often bedaubed with paint and antifouling, our eager-beaver expressions and our hearty one-of-the-lads manner. We've been known to swap dubious jokes and try to match our menfolk drink for drink, and then lead the company in late-night singsongs of rousing sea-shanties involving a great deal of whooping and back-slapping.

My own fond belief that I was striking a happy medium between these sailing stereotypes was shattered when a group of us was reminiscing about our summer cruises.

95

"Hey, do you remember that superwoman type we saw at Stornoway?" one of the skippers asked his crew. "The one with a laugh like a gannet who looked as if she was wearing her lifejacket *under* her jumper?"

"Oh yes," they grinned, waving their pints. "You could see the deck bending when she walked for'ard and she had biceps on her like a Japanese wrestler."

"And then," another continued, almost choking at the memory, "when he told her to let go the anchor, she tossed the darned thing in overarm!" And they all rocked about with mirth, and so did I until one of them delivered the bombshell.

"And we all said," he sniggered, wiping away a tear, *"she reminded us of you, Les."*

I did my best, through tight lips, to join in the general hilarity but somehow my laughter didn't ring as true as theirs as inwardly I pledged myself to frilly blouses, low-calorie meals and large amounts of helpless femininity for at least a month.

But it's impossible to keep up a front for long. The sea has its own way of stripping away affectations. The glamour girls, somehow, can manage always to retain heads of expensively casual and glossy silken curls and hands with varnished nails of uniform length, but the rest of us, after only a few hours at sea, look as though we eked out our living by quayside herring gutting in a permanent gale.

Lastly, we must not forget the sailing superwomen, the single-handers and round-the-world skipperesses who, without appearing to think it anything unusual, set up records and sailing 'firsts' that make the toughest men green-eyed with jealousy. Certainly their achievements put them forever on a plane apart from us lesser mortals, but we can at least derive some comfort from the thought that even they had to start somewhere. In their early days, I bet they lurched from blunder to blunder, from embarrassment to near-disaster just as I did (and, let's be honest, still do from time to time).

The only difference is that *they* elected to keep quiet about it.